the Soy for Health cookbook

the
Soy for Health
cookbook

recipes with style and taste

Kurumi Hayter

TIME
LIFE
BOOKS

Alexandria, Virginia

Time-Life Books is a division of Time Life Inc.
Time-Life is a trademark of Time Warner Inc. and affiliated companies.

TIME LIFE INC.
Chairman and Cheif Executive Officer: Jim Nelson
President and Cheif Operating Officer: Steven Janas
Senior Executive Vice President and Cheif Operations Officer: Mary Davis Holt
Senior Vice President and Cheif Financial Officer: Christopher Hearing

TIME-LIFE BOOKS
President: Larry Jellen
Senior Vice President, New Markets: Bridget Boel
Vice President, Home and Hearth Markets: Nicholas M. DiMarco
Vice President, Content Development: Jennifer L. Pearce

TIME-LIFE TRADE PUBLISHING
Vice President and Publisher: Neil S. Levin
Senior Sales Director: Richard J. Vreeland
Director, Marketing and Publicity: Inger Forland
Director of Trade Sales: Dana Hobson
Director of Custom Publishing: John Lalor
Director of Rights and Licensing: Olga Vezeris

THE TOFU FOR HEALTH COOKBOOK
Director of New Product Development: Carolyn M. Clark
New Product Development Manager: Lori A. Woehrle
Senior Editor: Linda Bellamy
Director of Design: Kate L. McConnell
Project Editor: Jennie Halfant

This book was designed and produced by
Quintet Publishing Limited
6 Blundell Street
London N7 7BH

Senior Project Editor: Laura Price
Editor: Margaret Gilbey
Nutritionist: Fiona Hunter
Art Directors: Labeena Ishaque, Sharanjit Dhol
Designer: James Lawrence
Photographer: Frank Adam
Home Economist: Jules Beresford

Creative Director: Richard Dewing

Typeset in Great Britain by Central Southern Typesetters, Eastbourne
Manufactured in Hong Kong by Regent Publishing Services Ltd.
Printed in China by Leefung-Asco Printers Ltd.

10 9 8 7 6 5 4 3 2 1

School and library distribution by Time-Life Education, P.O. Box 85026, Richmond, Virginia 23285-5026.

Library of Congress Cataloging-in-Publication Data available upon request:
Librarian, Time-Life Books
2000 Duke Street
Alexandria, Virginia 22314

ISBN 0-7370-1624-8

Contents

INTRODUCTION

The statistics speak for themselves—the little soybean is big in every way. In 1998, in the United States of America (the world's top producer) over 80 million acres were planted with soybeans, yielding a crop of over 70 million tons. World-wide, the soybean accounts for over half of all oilseed production, making it one of the most dominant agricultural commodities. The soybean has a long history—records show its cultivation in China as long ago as 3000 BC. Originally an Asian foodstuff, soy was imported to Europe in the sixteenth century but failed due to climatic and soil conditions. Soy arrived in the United States as ballast aboard clipper ships—and never looked back. Under cultivation, soy is a frost-tender annual, the beans maturing in 70 to 80 days. The plants reach about three feet (one meter) in height. The beans themselves are borne two or three to a pod.

The soybean finds its way into all kinds of food, from being processed into products such as tofu, tempeh, and soy sauce to being used as an additive in many of today's processed foods as a flavor enhancer and nutrient to being a major constituent of much animal feed. Around two-thirds of all manufactured foods contain ingredients derived from soy. Soybeans are highly versatile—they can be eaten whole after boiling or roasting, transformed into soy oil (better known as vegetable oil), lecithin, soy protein concentrate, textured soy protein, and many other derivatives. The list includes eda-mame (green vegetable soybeans), hydrolyzed vegetable protein (HVP), soy-based infant formula, miso, natto, soy ice cream, soy cheese, soy milk, soy yogurt, soy bran, soy flour, soy grits, soy protein concentrate, textured vegetable protein (TVP), soy sauce, soy margarine, tempeh, tofu, and yuba. Soybeans also find their way into a wide range of nonfood products such as detergents, soap, and some plastics.

Given that the little bean is so ubiquitous, it is surprising that the great nutritional and health benefits it offers are not more widely known. The section below deals with what the soybean can offer those seeking a healthier food style. In this book, I have tried to appeal to a broad cross section of readers. The soy products have been chosen not only for their adaptability to a wide range of recipes, both Western and Asian in origin, but also for their easy availability.

BELOW Soy beans

NUTRITION AND HEALTH

It is hard to think of any other common, widely used foodstuff that provides as many benefits as the soybean. The irony is that soy is used as a "bulking" or emulsifying agent in 70 percent of processed foods and is probably the most widely nutritious ingredient in them.

The "goodies" that soy can provide are many. It is the most complete form of high-

quality vegetable protein available. Its digestibility is similar to dairy milk protein, which is unusual as most vegetable protein is less digestible than animal protein. Soy protein is high in essential amino acids, especially lysine, and in this respect is again very similar to the profile of animal proteins such as meat and eggs.

It is a significant source of calcium. A half-cup of beans provides approximately 50 percent of the calcium of a half-cup of full cream milk. Soy milk, in many respects, is similar in nutritional value to low-fat dairy milk.

Soy contains useful levels of folic acid and is a good source of iron, potassium, and magnesium. It also contains moderate quantities of vitamins B_2, B_3, B_{12}, and D.

Being a plant product, soy contains no cholesterol and can even contribute to the lowering of blood cholesterol. In the United States, the Food and Drug Administration (FDA) is even proposing that foods that contain soy protein will be permitted to be labeled with the claim that these products can help reduce the risk of heart disease, "as part of a diet low in saturated fat and cholesterol."

Soy contains high concentrations of several compounds that exhibit anti-carcinogenic action, including isoflavones (which are found in far greater quantity in soy than any other foodstuff), protease inhibitors, and phytic acid. Isoflavones are also proven to have favorable effects on blood vessel function and reduce the risk of osteoporosis.

Soy is also high in polyunsaturated fats, the essential omega-3 fatty acids, both linoleic and linolenic, but is also low in saturated fats. It is a good source of fiber and, in all its forms, is low in calories.

A major source of nonnutrient compounds called phytoestrogens, soy contains quantities of around 3 milligrams per 100 grams of raw beans. Research has demonstrated that one of these phytoestrogens, genistein, inhibits the growth of cells that can clog arteries and may even help in the prevention of blood clots.

Finally, soy contains only traces of sodium and is therefore useful for those on a sodium-reduced diet.

Not only is soy healthy and nutritious, it is an easily digested food. Because of its high nutritional value, especially in terms of the protein it provides, soy can form an essential foundation of either a vegan or vegetarian diet regime. But even nonvegetarians can benefit from the addition of soy to their daily diet as a part replacement for other sources of protein. Soy can also be used in combination with meat to provide the fiber that animal protein lacks.

LACTOSE (DAIRY) INTOLERANCE

Lactose or milk intolerance is a widespread problem. Lactose intolerance is the inability to digest significant amounts of lactose, which is the predominant sugar contained in milk. This is caused by deficiency of an enzyme, lactase, which is

ABOVE Soy bacon

normally produced in the intestine. It is estimated that 50 million American adults are lactose intolerant. Some races are more widely affected than others. As many as 75 percent of all African-American, Jewish, and Native American adults, and 90 percent of Asian-American adults are lactose intolerant. The condition is least common among people of northern European descent.

Lactose intolerance is most severe in older women and in children born with the intolerance. In many cases, these groups must avoid milk and foods made with milk altogether. However, a carefully chosen diet can reduce symptoms and protect future health. Soy, and in particular soy milk, is widely available as a milk substitute. Certain brands offer calcium-enriched soy milk variants especially developed to provide an effective soy milk substitute for sufferers of lactose intolerance. For lactose-intolerant infants, soy milk, with additives to mimic exactly the nutritional profile of breast milk, is now widely available.

ABOVE Soy milk and yogurt

PREVENTION AGAINST HEART DISEASE

Heart disease is one of the leading causes of death in the Western world and kills one million people a year in the United States alone. In the United Kingdom, it is thought that as many as 20 percent of the population suffer from dangerously high levels of certain dangerous cholesterol variants. There are several causes of heart disease, all linked to lifestyle, but diet is known to be the principal non-hereditary factor. High blood cholesterol levels increase the risk for atherosclerosis, which is the underlying cause of heart disease and heart attacks. Both saturated fat and cholesterol consumed in the diet increase blood cholesterol levels. There has been much examination and debate of the role soy plays in reducing the risk of heart disease. It has been known for many years that soy foods, although rich in protein, are low in saturated fat and free of cholesterol. The fat in soy is mostly polyunsaturated, the kind that does not raise blood cholesterol levels. So substituting other sources of protein with soy protein to some degree should contribute positively to the maintenance of a healthy level of cholesterol. More than 50 independent research projects have demonstrated that the protein in soy foods acts directly to lower high levels of blood LDL cholesterol by 10 to 15 percent. The same, albeit reduced, effect has been noted in subjects who already enjoy low blood cholesterol levels. Although this does not seem a great reduction, it can reduce the risk of a heart attack by 20 to 30 percent. This is because soy protein not only reduces cholesterol but also prevents the oxidation of cholesterol—it is only oxidized cholesterol that can damage the heart arteries. Uniquely, soy protein does not reduce the beneficial HDL cholesterol.

ABOVE Soy sausages

It is also now becoming recognized that the isoflavone content of soy foods—found in meaningful amounts only in soy products such as tofu and soy milk—also has a positive effect on lowering the risk of coronary disease by preventing oxidation. Isoflavones are also thought to improve blood vessel function.

ABOVE Firm tofu

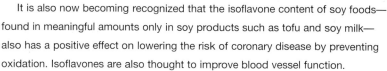

About 25 grams of soy protein per day may be enough to lower cholesterol. This is the amount of soy protein found in just one cup of soybeans. Higher amounts of soy protein (25 to 50 grams) are likely to produce even greater decreases. Soy protein appears to be effective whether you use it in place of other protein foods in your diet or if you simply add it to your existing diet.

The National Health Service in Italy is so convinced of the benefits of soy that it provides soy free of charge to physicians for the treatment of high blood cholesterol.

If more evidence of the proven benefits of soy were needed, on October 26, 1999, the United States FDA permitted use of health claims about the role of soy protein in reducing the risk of coronary heart disease to be printed on the labels of foods containing soy protein. This decision was based on the FDA's conclusion that foods containing soy protein, when included in a diet low in saturated fat and cholesterol, reduces the risk of heart disease by lowering blood cholesterol levels.

PREVENTION AGAINST CANCER

The incidence of prostate, breast, ovarian, and other forms of cancers is low in populations with a high dietary intake of soy products, such as those of East Asia. It has been suggested that phytoestrogens, derived from soy, act to prevent the development and spread of cancerous tumors. Although research is still not conclusive in scientific terms, enough laboratory investigation has been carried out to suggest that they do indeed inhibit the growth of cancerous cells.

PREVENTION OF OTHER DISORDERS

Studies have demonstrated that an increased dietary consumption of the phytoestrogens, daidzein and genistein found in soy, alleviate the symptoms of menopause, such as hot flashes, loss of bone mineral density, and loss of bone mineral content.

ABOVE Soy sauce

Osteoporosis is a problem of growing concern all over the world. The use of soy products in Asian countries in particular has become associated with lower incidence of osteoporosis and related problems such bone fractures. Studies have shown that the isoflavones contained in soy have a booster effect on the body's ability to absorb and take up calcium.

It is clear that eating a soy-rich diet has significant health benefits for both young and old, healthy and infirm. Low in fat and calories, high in protein, isoflavones, calcium, vitamins, and fiber, the inclusion of significant amounts of soy products in the diet provides short-term effects such as a reduction in cholesterol and obesity and long-term prevention against the illnesses outlined above.

HOW TO USE THIS BOOK

Given the health benefits of incorporating soy food products into your eating habits, it is important to know how much soy will produce positive health results. In this book, my objective is to give the broadest possible audience the chance to enjoy the benefits of this nutritional gem in those forms that are widely available. Therefore, I have included both dishes, which would include a soy ingredient as a matter of course, and other recipes that are well known in a non-soy context, and in which I have replaced an ingredient or ingredients with soy alternatives. In still other recipes, I have tried to provide a few innovative dishes based on soy products and have been subjective in choosing some soy products, such as soy sausages, which I think are a good substitute for the traditional meat variety.

The following guidelines should be seen as general indications and are divided into recommendations for both general and special-purpose use. For those in good general health, six to eight servings of soy protein per week is ideal. This would provide approximately 8 to 12 grams of soy protein a day and 16 to 22 milligrams of soy isoflavones. This could be obtained, for example, from one cup of soy milk a day, or two servings of tofu four times weekly.

For those at risk of heart disease and those with high hereditary probability of heart disease, osteoporosis, or diabetes, 12 to 14 servings of soy protein per week is recommended. This would provide approximately 14 to 18 grams of soy protein, with 28 to 36 milligrams of soy isoflavones.

For those with coronary heart disease or osteoporosis, a target consumption is 18 to 20 servings of soy protein per week. This would provide approximately 22 to 28 grams of soy protein daily with 44 to 56 milligrams of soy isoflavones daily. For persons wishing to follow this, the consumption of a soy powder dietary supplement is recommended.

FOR YOUR CUPBOARD

Deep-fried beancurd pouch (Abura-age) Made from soybeans and deep fried. It is light brown in color and has a spongelike texture. Abura-age is a Japanese specialty and is mainly available from Asian stores.

Bonito flakes (Katsuo bushi) Traditionally, katsuo bushi was sold in dried blocks from which shavings were taken with a knife or scraper. These days, ready-shaved flakes of dried bonito fish are available in sealed plastic envelopes in a packet. Katsuo bushi is one of the essential ingredients used in making Japanese broth. It is sold in Asian stores and health food shops.

Black bean sauce A widely used Chinese ingredient, black bean sauce is made from a mixture of fermented black soybeans with salt and a number of spices. The sauce has a rich aroma and a tangy, salty taste. Both whole black beans and black bean paste are available from Chinese stores and even some large supermarkets. Black beans can be kept up to six months, refrigerated.

Chili bean sauce This hot chili paste is made from a combination of fermented soybeans, chile, and spices. The strength of chili bean sauce varies quite considerably depending on the brand you choose. It is available from large supermarkets and Chinese food stores.

Dried hijiki or black seaweed Hijiki is a dried seaweed eaten in Japan. Like other seaweeds, hijiki is rich in minerals and low in calories. Dried hijiki has to be soaked in water about 30 minutes before use. Available from Asian and health food stores.

Dried kelp (Konbu) Kelp is another kind of seaweed and is used in making Japanese stock as well as for cooking. It is a good source of iodine and other trace elements. Konbu is available from Asian food stores or large supermarkets and health food stores. Konbu comes in stiff strips and should be wiped clean before use—washing konbu under the faucet reduces the mineral content.

Fish sauce (Nam pla) Fish sauce has a very distinct aroma and a salty taste. It is one of the mainstays of Thai cooking and is also widely used in the rest of South Asian cuisine. Available from Asian food stores or large supermarkets.

Kaffir lime leaves (Bai makrat) Kaffir lime leaves are used as an herb in their native Thailand and impart a strong lemon flavor. Dried kaffir lime leaves are widely available and do not need to be soaked before use.

Mirin Mirin is one of the key ingredients in Japanese cooking. It contains a very low level of alcohol; mirin is only used to sweeten foods, not for consumption as a drink. Mirin can be bought from Asian food stores or large supermarkets.

Miso Miso is a paste of fermented soybeans, rice (or barley), salt, and water. Miso has a rich, salty flavor, and is widely used in Japanese and Korean cooking. The intensity of the flavor of miso can be judged by its color—the darker the paste, the richer its flavor.

It can be used in soups, stews, dressings, marinades, dips, and toppings. The fermentation period for miso can be anything between three months and three years. Miso is available in Asian stores and health food stores, and is becoming more widely available in supermarkets.

Nori seaweed sheet Nori is made from dried and chopped purple laver seaweed, rolled into paper-thin sheets. Its most typical use in Japan is as a wrapper for sushi. Nori has to be kept in an airtight container to keep it fresh. It is available from large supermarkets or Asian food stores.

Shaoxing rice wine Shaoxing is a Chinese rice wine, widely used for cooking as well as drinking in China, though as a wine it is probably too sweet for Western tastes. Shaoxing wine is made from sticky rice, yeast, and water. Shaoxing wine will keep, sealed, for a month.

Shiitake mushroom These large, brown mushrooms are the most commonly used mushrooms in Asian cooking. Both fresh and dried shiitake mushrooms are available. The dried form has the stronger taste.

Soy bacon Soy bacon is made from a mixture of soy oil and soy protein, starch, salt, and a gelling agent such as carrageen. Soy bacon has a taste not unlike true bacon though many brands add a good deal of coloring.

Soy cheese Soy cheese is made from soy milk and/or tofu, soybean oil, and salt. The recipes in this book use an unflavored soy cheese that can be compared to mozzarella. Other soy cheeses have added flavorings such as red and green bell peppers, spices, and herbs. Soy cheese may also include an ingredient such as carrageen to improve texture.

Soy margarine Soy margarine is made from emulsified soy oil, typically combined with palm oil and salt. Some brands include other flavorings. Soy margarine has a nongreasy texture and contains no cholesterol. Used in cooking, soy margarine makes for lighter, less oily versions of dishes, particularly where it is used as a substitute for butter.

Soy milk Soy milk is a healthy alternative to dairy milk and especially valuable for those who suffer from lactose intolerance. Soy milk has a texture indistinguishable from milk, though its flavor is less "fatty." Soy milk is made from ground soybeans, mixed with water, then cooked and filtered. Soy milk is now available in many supermarkets and all health food stores, from a variety of manufacturers, and in a wide variety of forms. Once opened, soy milk will stay fresh in the refrigerator for five to seven days. Along with its application in recipes as a milk substitute, soy milk can be used in simpler ways, such as on cereal or in milk shakes.

Soy breakfast sausage links Soy sausages look like the real thing but taste quite different. They are normally heavily herbed and spiced to provide them with flavor and, as a result, many people find it easy to give up the "real thing" in their favor. Soy sausages should only be cut or sliced after cooking when they will be firmer and less likely to crumble.

Soy sauce Soy sauce is made from soybeans, water, flour, and sea salt and is left to age for between four months and three years. Chinese, Korean, and Japanese soy sauces have very different flavors so never use Chinese soy sauce in Japanese cooking or vice versa. Soy sauce can be found in most health food stores and supermarkets.

Sushi vinegar (Su) Sushi vinegar is a clear-colored liquid that has a rather sweet flavor and is mainly used for making sushi rice. Sushi vinegar can also be used for making dressings or marinades. Ready-made sushi vinegar is available from large supermarkets and Asian food stores.

Tempeh Tempeh is a traditional Indonesian food, made from soybeans that have been cooked, roughly ground, and then fermented. Tempeh has a chewy consistency and an almost nutty flavor. Tempeh is very firm and can be handled without fear of it crumbling and can be cooked in a variety of ways. Tempeh is still found almost exclusively in health food stores. It can last for up to a year retained in plastic wrap, but should be eaten within two to three weeks once opened. Tempeh is a good source of fiber and high-quality protein, and is low in saturated fats.

Tofu Tofu, or soybean curd, is made from curdled soy milk. Tofu itself is quite tasteless, though its high absorbency means it can be readily marinated for flavor. Its softness and mildness make it an ideal infant food and even a good source of nutrition for the elderly or infirm. Tofu varies with regard to its consistency as follows:
Extra-firm tofu: contains the lowest water content and is quite robust, enabling it to be sliced or diced for frying or boiling. Extra-firm tofu also has the highest protein and fat content.
Firm tofu: though not as firm as the above, it is still solid enough to be cut.
Soft tofu: much softer and therefore suitable for dressings and sauces.
Silken tofu: has a finer, smoother structure, hence the name. Silken tofu is available in firm and soft varieties but is not as firm as its coarser relatives.

Tofu can be found in most supermarkets, though the freshest tofu is still normally only available from Asian food stores.

Fresh tofu should be used within one or two days of purchase. Unopened it can be stored in the refrigerator for three to five days. Carton-packed tofu is viable for longer if unopened.

Basic recipes

THESE BASIC RECIPES ARE STAPLES THAT OCCUR IN MANY
OF THE RECIPES IN THIS BOOK.

vegetable broth

IF TIME IS LIMITED, BOUILLON CUBES OR GRANULES CAN
BE USED AS AN ALTERNATIVE.

MAKES ABOUT 5 CUPS

5½ cups water

1 clove garlic, peeled and sliced

1 medium onion, peeled and
   roughly chopped

1 large carrot, roughly chopped

2 celery ribs, roughly chopped

½ leek, roughly chopped

1 bouquet garni (parsley, thyme,
   bay leaves, and rosemary)

2 black peppercorns

1 Put all the ingredients into a large pan. Bring
to a boil and simmer for 40 to 50 minutes.

2 Skim off the surface occasionally. When
ready, strain the broth. Refrigerate when cool
and use within 2 to 3 days. Alternatively, it can
be frozen in batches and used when required.

nutrition facts	
energy	11 cal
	45 kJ
protein	0.5 g
fat	0 g
of which saturated	0 g
carbohydrate	2 g
fiber	0 g
cholesterol	0 mg
sodium	10 mg

chicken broth

SUPERIOR HOMEMADE BROTHS CAN REALLY MAKE A
DIFFERENCE TO A DISH.

MAKES ABOUT 5 CUPS

5½ cups water

1½ lb chicken bones or wings

1 onion, cut into quarters

1 small carrot, roughly chopped

1 celery rib, roughly chopped

2 bouquet garni

4 black peppercorns

1 Put all the ingredients into a pan.

2 Bring to a boil and simmer for 50 to
60 minutes. Skim the surface occasionally.
Discard the bones and vegetables, and strain
the liquid through a fine-mesh strainer.

nutrition facts	
energy	18 cal
	73 kJ
protein	3 g
fat	1 g
of which saturated	0 g
carbohydrate	0 g
fiber	1 g
cholesterol	14 mg
sodium	112 mg

japanese **fish** broth

MAKES ABOUT 5 CUPS

5 cups water

6-in strip of dried kelp, wiped
    clean

⅓ cup dried bonito flakes

THE FOUNDATION STONE OF MANY JAPANESE RECIPES. THE FIRST BROTH PREPARED IS CLASSED AS "PREMIER" JAPANESE BROTH. YOU CAN RECYCLE THE INGREDIENTS ALREADY USED TO MAKE "STANDARD" BROTH. FOR CONVENIENCE, INSTANT JAPANESE BROTH IS AVAILABLE FROM MOST ASIAN FOOD STORES AND SUPERMARKETS.

1 Without cutting all the way through, cut the strip of kelp widthwise several times to give it a fringed look. Put the water and kelp in a pan and bring to a boil over a medium heat. When the water starts to boil, remove the kelp.

2 Add the bonito flakes and bring the water back to a boil over a low heat. When the water starts to boil again, turn off the heat. Wait until bonito flakes sink to the bottom of the pan, then strain the liquid through a fine-mesh strainer.

nutrition facts	
energy	11 cal
	45 kJ
protein	2.5 g
fat	0 g
of which saturated	0 g
carbohydrate	0 g
fiber	0 g
cholesterol	00 mg
sodium	1093 mg

Tips

• To make "standard" Japanese broth, put 1 oz dried bonito flakes and the used kelp and bonito flakes in a pan containing 5 cups water. Bring the liquid to a boil and simmer for 5 to 6 minutes over a low heat. Strain as above.

• To use the instant Japanese broth, dissolve 1 heaping teaspoonful of bouillon granules in 3 cups of hot water.

japanese **vegan** broth

MAKES ABOUT 5 CUPS

5 cups water

1 dried shiitake mushroom

8-in strip of dried kelp, wiped

FOR THOSE WISHING TO ADHERE TO A VEGAN REGIME, THIS BROTH IS PREPARED WITHOUT THE ADDITION OF BONITO FLAKES.

1 Without cutting all the way through, cut the strip of kelp as above. Soak the shiitake mushrooms and the dried kelp in a bowl of water.

2 Remove the mushrooms after 1 hour and take out the kelp after 2 to 3 hours.

nutrition facts	
energy	16 cal
	65 kJ
protein	0.5 g
fat	0 g
of which saturated	0 g
carbohydrate	0 g
fiber	0 g
cholesterol	0 mg
sodium	11 mg

cooking **rice**

THE METHOD OF RICE COOKING DEPENDS ON THE VARIETY OF RICE
YOU USE. THE FINISHED ARTICLE IS ALSO QUITE DISTINCT. GIVEN
HERE ARE TWO DIFFERENT WAYS OF COOKING RICE. THE COOKING
TIME WILL VARY SLIGHTLY DEPENDING ON THE AMOUNT OF RICE
PREPARED. I FIND THAT MANY PEOPLE SKIMP ON THE WASHING
STAGE—IT REALLY IS WORTH THE TIME SPENT TO PRODUCE CLEAN
GRAINS READY FOR COOKING. I HAVE INCLUDED THE TYPICAL
WESTERN AND ASIAN METHODS OF RINSING—I MAKE NO JUDGMENT
AS TO WHICH IS BEST!

long-grain rice

SERVES 4

1¾ cups long-grain rice

3¾ cups water

1 Wash the rice in a strainer with cold, running water.
Repeat five or six times. Bring the water to a boil then
add the rice. Simmer for 10 to 12 minutes uncovered.
2 Drain the rice in the strainer and rinse with boiling
water. Shake the rice lightly to produce the characteristic
fluffy texture.

nutrition facts	
energy	360 cal
	1502 kJ
protein	7 g
fat	0.5 g
of which saturated	0 g
carbohydrate	80 g
fiber	0 g
cholesterol	0 mg
sodium	0 mg

short-grain rice

SERVES 4

1¾ cups short-grain rice, such
as the Japanese brands now
available

3¾ cups water

1 Put the rice in a pan with water. Swirl the grains with
your fingers until the water becomes cloudy, then drain.
Repeat this a few times before draining in a strainer.
2 Put the rice and water back in the pan. Bring to a boil
and simmer for 12 to15 minutes over a low heat with the
lid on.
3 When the rice is cooked, turn off the heat, but keep the
lid on for 5 minutes. All the water should be absorbed and
the rice should be sticky.

nutrition facts	
energy	360 cal
	1502 kJ
protein	7 g
fat	0.5 g
of which saturated	0 g
carbohydrate	80 g
fiber	0 g
cholesterol	0 mg
sodium	0 mg

short crust **pastry**

MAKES 2½ CUPS

2 cups self-rising flour, sifted

A pinch of salt

½ cup soy margarine, chilled

3 to 4 Tbsp water

ANOTHER EXAMPLE OF HOW SOY PRODUCTS CAN BE INTEGRATED INTO TRADITIONAL FOOD. SOY MARGARINE GIVES A LIGHTER, LESS GREASY PASTRY AND IS SUITABLE FOR BOTH VEGETARIANS AND VEGANS.

1 Sift the flour and salt in a bowl. Blend the margarine into the flour until the mixture looks like breadcrumbs.

2 Stir the water in and lightly knead to form the dough. Wrap with plastic wrap and rest it in a refrigerator for at least 30 minutes.

nutrition facts	
energy	1563 cal
	6539 kJ
protein	20 g
fat	94 g
of which saturated	19 g
carbohydrate	170 g
fiber	7 g
cholesterol	2 mg
sodium	1558 mg

soy **béchamel sauce**

MAKES ABOUT 1 CUP

1¼ cups soy milk, unsweetened

3 sprigs of parsley

4 black peppercorns

1 slice of onion

1 bay leaf

A pinch of ground nutmeg or mace

2 Tbsp soy margarine

¼ cup all-purpose flour

Salt and black pepper

A LIGHTER, HEALTHIER VERSION OF THE CLASSIC FRENCH SAUCE.

1 Put the milk, parsley, peppercorns, onion, bay leaf, and the nutmeg in a pan. Slowly bring to boiling point, and simmer over a low heat for 4 to 5 minutes. Strain and allow to cool.

2 Melt the margarine in a pan over a low heat. Add the flour and blend in well. Stir in the cooled milk a little at a time, mixing well with a spoon each time you add the milk.

3 Repeat this process until all the milk has been used up. Season with salt and pepper.

nutrition facts	
energy	405 cal
	1679 kJ
protein	11 g
fat	31 g
of which saturated	6 g
carbohydrate	22 g
fiber	1 g
cholesterol	1 mg
sodium	300 mg

1 soups and stews

Delicious, warming, and filling, the soups and stews in this section are truly inspiring in the use of soy products. From meat substitutes to low-fat options, soy offers a range of super soup and stew ideas. The range of products is surprising. These dishes make the best use of soy breakfast sausage links, textured vegetable protein, red and white miso, tofu, and soy cheese. Once you feel confident, you can use any of the ingredients to experiment with and add an extra twist to your own favorite recipes.

LEFT mixed beans and pasta soup (page 22)

pumpkin soup

A TRADITIONAL "WINTER WARMER" MADE OVER TO FIT A LOW-CALORIE, LOW-FAT LIFESTYLE.

SERVES 4

2 Tbsp soy margarine

1 medium onion, sliced

1 potato, peeled and chopped

½ pumpkin, peeled, seeded, and chopped

3¾ cups water

1 cup soy milk

Salt and white pepper

4 Tbsp soy cream

Chives, for garnish

1 Melt the margarine in a pan, add the onion, potato, and pumpkin, and sauté for 2 minutes. Add the water and bring to a boil. Simmer for 30 minutes.

2 Allow the liquid to cool slightly, then purée it in a food processor.

3 Bring the liquid back to the pan and add the soy milk. Season with salt and pepper, and reheat.

4 Pour the soy cream over the soup and garnish with the chives.

nutrition facts	
energy	215 cal
	900 kJ
protein	5.5 g
fat	9 g
of which saturated	3 g
carbohydrate	30 g
fiber	4 g
cholesterol	9 mg
sodium	86 mg

creamed **carrot** soup

SERVES 4

2 Tbsp soy margarine

1 medium onion, roughly
chopped

1 celery rib, roughly chopped

1 tomato, roughly chopped

4 large carrots, peeled and
chopped

3 cups water

Salt and black pepper

½ cup light soy cream

Basil leaves, for garnish

THIS SIMPLE, NOURISHING SOUP IS BEST SIMPLY SERVED WITH FRESH BAKED BREAD. IT CAN BE EASILY ADJUSTED TO MAKE A MORE FILLING MEAL, HOWEVER. TRY ADDING ONE CUP OF MACARONI OR FARFALLE BEFORE SIMMERING THE SOUP TO MAKE A FILLING, WARMING MEAL.

1 Melt the margarine in a pan, then add the onion, celery, tomato, and carrots, and sauté for 3 minutes.

2 Add the water and bring to a boil. Simmer for 30 minutes. Season with the salt and pepper.

3 Allow the soup to cool slightly, then purée until smooth in a blender or food processor.

4 Return the soup to the pan, add the cream, and reheat. Garnish with the basil leaves and serve.

nutrition facts	
energy	155 cal
	636 kJ
protein	2 g
fat	10 g
of which saturated	2 g
carbohydrate	14 g
fiber	3.5 g
cholesterol	10 mg
sodium	90 mg

mixed beans
and pasta soup

A HEALTHY SOUP WITH A MEDITERRANEAN FLAVOR THAT IS
EQUALLY DELICIOUS CHILLED AS A SUMMER'S DAY APPETIZER.

SERVES 4

2 Tbsp extra-virgin olive oil

1 medium onion, chopped

2 cloves garlic, chopped

1 zucchini, chopped

½ tsp chili powder

1 tsp coriander

4 Tbsp canned red kidney beans

4 Tbsp canned or frozen
   soybeans

4 Tbsp canned flageolet beans

5 cups vegetable or chicken
   broth

Salt and black pepper

1 tomato, peeled and chopped

½ cup small pasta shapes

4-6 cilantro leaves

Basil leaves, for garnish

1 Heat the oil in a pan. Add the onion, garlic, and zucchini, and sauté for 3 minutes or until softened.

2 Add the chili powder, coriander, beans, and broth. Season with salt and pepper, then simmer for 30 minutes, covered.

3 Add the tomato, pasta, and cilantro, and simmer for a further 10 minutes.

4 Garnish with the basil leaves and serve.

nutrition facts	
energy	200 cal
	856 kJ
protein	11 g
fat	8 g
of which saturated	1 g
carbohydrate	22 g
fiber	7 g
cholesterol	0 mg
sodium	419 mg

sweetcorn soup

THIS LIGHT, NON-OILY SOUP IS DELICIOUS SERVED WITH FRESH
BAKED FRENCH BREAD.

SERVES 4

2 Tbsp soy margarine

2 medium onions, sliced

2 cups canned corn kernels

3 cups vegetable or chicken
   broth

1 cup soy milk

Salt and black pepper

Croûtons, for garnish

1 Melt the soy margarine in a pan. Add the
onion and corn, and fry for 2 to 3 minutes.
2 Add the broth, bring to a boil, and simmer
for 30 minutes. Turn off the heat.
3 When the soup has cooled, purée it in a food
processor until smooth.
4 Return the soup to the pan, add the soy
milk, and season with salt and pepper to taste.
Garnish with the croûtons.

nutrition facts	
energy	200 cal
	834 kJ
protein	6 g
fat	8 g
of which saturated	1.5 g
carbohydrate	27 g
fiber	2 g
cholesterol	0 mg
sodium	659 mg

asparagus and potato
in miso soup

MISO COMES IN A VARIETY OF COLORS AND ITS STRENGTH CAN
BE JUDGED BY THE DEPTH OF COLOR. THE WHITE MISO USED IN
THIS RECIPE IS THE MILDEST IN TASTE AND THEREFORE VERY
WELL MATCHED TO THE DELICATE TASTE OF THE ASPARAGUS.

SERVES 4

3¾ cups Japanese fish or vegan
   broth (see page 13)

8 asparagus, trimmed and cut
   into 1-in lengths

14-16 baby potatoes, peeled and
   cut into ½-in slices

½ medium onion, sliced

3 Tbsp white miso

1 Put the broth, asparagus, potatoes, and
onion in a pan. Bring to a boil and simmer for
about 8 minutes or until the potatoes are
softened.
2 Stir the miso into the soup until dissolved.
When it returns to boiling, turn off the heat and
serve hot.

nutrition facts	
energy	52 cal
	220 kJ
protein	4 g
fat	1 g
of which saturated	0 g
carbohydrate	7 g
fiber	1 g
cholesterol	0 mg
sodium	593 mg

tennel and
soy cheese soup

SOY CHEESE RESEMBLES A FIRM MOZZARELLA AND THOUGH THE TASTES ARE DIFFERENT, THEY ARE EQUIVALENT IN TERMS OF THEIR MILDNESS. SOY CHEESE IS A GREAT SOURCE OF FAT-FREE PROTEIN, MAKING IT AN IDEAL CONTRIBUTION TO ANY DIET.

SERVES 4

2 Tbsp soy margarine

1 clove garlic, peeled and finely chopped

1 leek, sliced

2 large fennel bulbs, chopped

5 cups vegetable or chicken broth (see page 12)

Salt and black pepper

4 Tbsp grated soy cheese

Fresh chopped parsley, for garnish

1 Melt the margarine in a pan, then add the garlic, leek, and fennel. Sauté for 5 minutes.

2 Add the broth and bring to a boil. Simmer for 30 minutes. Season to taste with the salt and pepper.

3 Allow the soup to cool slightly, then purée until smooth in a blender or food processor.

4 Return the soup to the pan and reheat. Add the cheese and garnish with the parsley.

nutrition facts	
energy	120 cal
	485 kJ
protein	11 g
fat	10 g
of which saturated	1 g
carbohydrate	2.5 g
fiber	2.5 g
cholesterol	0 mg
sodium	50 mg

mussels in clear broth

A CLASSIC JAPANESE BROTH. FOR A LIGHT MEAL, SERVE WITH
JAPANESE RICE AND A FEW PICKLED VEGETABLES.

SERVES 4

2 Tbsp cress, washed, or ¼ cup
fine-chopped watercress

3¾ cups Japanese fish broth

16 mussels, washed

1 Tbsp Japanese rice wine

3 Tbsp white miso

1 Blanch the cress in a pan of boiling water for
1 minute.

2 Put the broth, mussels, and rice wine in a
pan. Bring to a boil and simmer until the
mussels open. Add the miso and stir until
dissolved. Remove any mussels that remain
unopened.

3 Put four mussels and a bunch of cress in
each bowl, then pour the soup in.

nutrition facts	
energy	35 cal
	150 kJ
protein	5 g
fat	1 g
of which saturated	0 g
carbohydrate	2 g
fiber	0 g
cholesterol	0 mg
sodium	412 mg

spinach and **deep-fried beancurd** in miso soup

BEANCURD IS ALSO KNOWN AS TOFU. THE JAPANESE DEEP FRY
IT AND CALL IT "ABURA-AGE," TYPICALLY STUFFING ABURA-
AGE POUCHES WITH STICKY RICE. ABURA-AGE IS A GOOD
PARTNER TO THE SPINACH USED IN THIS RECIPE.

SERVES 4

3¾ cups Japanese fish or vegan
broth

2 cups fresh spinach

1 beancurd pouch, halved and
sliced

3 Tbsp red miso

2 scallions, chopped

1 Put the broth, spinach, and beancurd in a
pan. Bring to a boil and simmer for about
4 minutes.

2 Dissolve the miso in the soup and add the
scallions. When it returns to boiling, turn off
the heat and serve hot.

nutrition facts	
energy	150 cal
	650 kJ
protein	5 g
fat	2 g
of which saturated	0 g
carbohydrate	5 g
fiber	2.5 g
cholesterol	15 mg
sodium	245 mg

soybeans and **vegetables** in miso stew

SERVES 4

2 Tbsp sesame oil

1¼ cups carrots, peeled and sliced diagonally

1 leek, sliced into ½-in pieces

5 baby potatoes, cut into ½-in slices

½ large white radish (daikan), peeled and cut into bite-size pieces

½ small rutabaga, peeled and cut into bite-size pieces

3 cups Japanese fish or vegan broth

3 cups canned or frozen soybeans, drained

4 Tbsp red miso

1 Tbsp Japanese soy sauce

2 Tbsp dry-fried sesame seeds

RED MISO HAS A RICH, EARTHY TASTE. IF YOU USE MISO REGULARLY, YOU WILL WANT TO ADJUST THE AMOUNT USED IN ACCORDANCE WITH YOUR PREFERENCE FOR ITS SALTY FLAVOR.

1 Heat the oil in a pan, then add the carrots, leek, potatoes, white radish, and rutabaga, and sauté for 5 minutes.

2 Add the Japanese broth and soybeans. Bring to a boil and simmer for 20 minutes.

3 Add the miso and soy sauce, and heat for 5 more minutes. Sprinkle with the sesame seeds and serve with a hot bowl of rice.

nutrition facts	
energy	360 cal
	1518 kJ
protein	20 g
fat	18 g
of which saturated	2 g
carbohydrate	32 g
fiber	10 g
cholesterol	0 mg
sodium	1000 mg

soy sausage and **bell pepper** stew

SERVES 4

2 Tbsp sunflower oil

8 soy breakfast sausage links

1 medium onion, sliced

1 red bell pepper, seeded and sliced

1 green bell pepper, seeded and sliced

1¾ cups button mushrooms, sliced

1 Tbsp all-purpose flour

2 cups canned tomatoes

2 Tbsp red wine vinegar

2 Tbsp Worcestershire sauce

2 Tbsp brown sugar

1 Tbsp mustard

1¼ cups vegetable or chicken broth

1 Tbsp chopped fresh parsley

Salt and black pepper

"HEARTY" USED TO BE A EUPHEMISM FOR "HIGH-FAT." THIS RECIPE GIVES A TRADITIONAL EUROPEAN PEASANT DISH A HEALTHY TWIST.

1 Heat 1 tablespoon of oil in a skillet and brown the sausages lightly. Add another tablespoon of oil to the pan and then add the onion, red and green bell peppers, and mushrooms, and sauté for 2 to 3 minutes.

2 Add the flour, then stir for 1 minute. Add the tomato, vinegar, Worcestershire sauce, sugar, and mustard, and stir well.

3 Add the broth and parsley, and bring to a boil. Simmer for 30 minutes. Season with salt and pepper. Serve with your choice of mashed potato, rice, or fettuccine.

nutrition facts	
energy	230 cal
	960 kJ
protein	11 g
fat	10 g
of which saturated	1 g
carbohydrate	25 g
fiber	3 g
cholesterol	0 mg
sodium	320 mg

soy patties in **goulash**

SERVES 4

4-oz package soy burgermix

1 small egg, beaten

½ cup water

3 Tbsp extra-virgin olive oil

1 onion, chopped

1 green bell pepper, seeded and sliced

2 Tbsp paprika

2 tsp caraway seeds

2 tsp all-purpose flour

7-oz can tomatoes

1 cup vegetable or chicken broth

1 Tbsp tomato paste

2 cups button mushrooms

12-14 baby potatoes, cut into halves

Salt and black pepper

TEXTURED VEGETABLE PROTEIN REALLY COMES INTO ITS OWN WHEN IT IS USED IN SOUPS AND STEWS. THE RESULT IS EVERY BIT AS WARMING AND FILLING AS A MEAT DISH.

1 To make the patties, put the burgermix, egg, and water into a bowl, mix, and allow to stand for 15 minutes, or follow the instructions on the package. Form the mix into small pattie shapes with your hands.

2 Heat the oil in a pan and lightly brown the patties on both sides. Set aside. Add the onion, bell pepper, paprika, caraway seeds, and flour, and sauté for 2 to 3 minutes.

3 Add the tomatoes and mix well. Add the broth, tomato paste, patties, mushrooms, and potatoes, and bring to a boil. Simmer for about 30 minutes. Season with salt and pepper to taste. Serve hot.

nutrition facts	
energy	330 cal
	1382 kJ
protein	16 g
fat	14 g
of which saturated	2 g
carbohydrate	36 g
fiber	3 g
cholesterol	59 mg
sodium	157 mg

2 salads and appetizers

The recipes in this section provide a culinary tour of terrific flavors drawing inspiration from Western, Thai, Indian, Levantine, Chinese, and Japanese favorites. With inspirational use of tempeh, tofu, and soybeans, these delicious healthy dishes create a range of tasty options. There's even a no-egg omelet to dress a classic Japanese appetizer.

LEFT tofu and tomato kabobs with arugula (page 44)

tofu salad with thai-style dressing

A FUSION OF EAST AND WEST, THE TOFU AND THAI DRESSING
ENHANCE THE TASTE AND TEXTURE OF THE BASIC SALAD DISH.

SERVES 4

½ cup baby corn, cut into halves

10 oz firm tofu, cut into ½-in cubes

1 cup shredded iceberg lettuce

1 carrot, peeled and shredded

½ green bell pepper, thinly sliced

6 cherry tomatoes, halved

1 shallot, sliced thin

3 Tbsp cilantro leaves

2 Tbsp roasted peanuts, roughly chopped

FOR THE THAI-STYLE DRESSING:

1 clove garlic, finely chopped

½ fresh small red chile

1 Tbsp freshly squeezed lime juice

2 tsp brown sugar

1 Tbsp fish sauce

2 Tbsp sunflower oil

1 Boil the baby corn in a pan of boiling water for 4 to 5 minutes, then drain. Blanch the tofu in another pan of boiling water and drain this.

2 In a bowl, mix the lettuce, carrot, bell pepper, tomatoes, shallot, cilantro, baby corn, and tofu.

3 Place the garlic, chile, lime juice, sugar, fish sauce, and oil in a jar, and shake well to mix. Pour the dressing over the salad and sprinkle with the peanuts just before serving.

nutrition facts	
energy	190 cal
	790 kJ
protein	10 g
fat	12 g
of which saturated	2 g
carbohydrate	11 g
fiber	3 g
cholesterol	0 mg
sodium	460 mg

fusilli and **soybean salad** with soy yogurt curry dressing

SOY YOGURT HAS A MUCH MILDER TASTE THAN THE ORGANIC DAIRY ORIGINAL. IN THIS DISH, I FIND THAT ITS BLANDNESS ALLOWS THE SPICES MORE "BREATHING SPACE" AND DELIVERS A CLEANER TASTE.

SERVES 4

4 cups dried fusilli

¾ cup green beans, cut into 1-in lengths

1 small avocado, pitted and diced

3 cups canned or frozen soybeans, drained

1 red bell pepper, seeded and chopped

4 Tbsp raisins

FOR THE SOY YOGURT CURRY DRESSING:

2 tsp curry powder

1 tsp ground cumin

8 Tbsp soy yogurt

8 Tbsp mayonnaise

3 Tbsp freshly squeezed lemon juice

Salt and black pepper

1 Cook the fusilli in a pan of boiling water until *al dente* (firm to the bite). Blanch the green beans in a pan of boiling water for 5 minutes and drain.

2 In a bowl, put the cooked fusilli, green beans, avocado, soybeans, bell pepper, and raisins. Add the curry powder, cumin, soy yogurt, mayonnaise, and lemon juice, then mix together.

3 Season with salt and pepper to taste. Serve cold.

nutrition facts	
energy	740 cal
	3086 kJ
protein	25 g
fat	39 g
of which saturated	6 g
carbohydrate	76 g
fiber	11 g
cholesterol	23 mg
sodium	157 mg

mixed **bean** salad

1 cup green beans, trimmed and
  cut into halves

6 Tbsp canned or frozen
  soybeans

4 Tbsp canned lima beans

4 Tbsp canned red kidney beans

1 shallot, sliced

Salt and black pepper

FOR THE DRESSING:

½ clove garlic, finely chopped

2 Tbsp freshly squeezed lemon
  juice

4 Tbsp extra-virgin olive oil

1 Tbsp chopped fresh parsley

2 medium tomatoes, sliced for
  decoration

Some black olives, for garnish

A GOOD BEAN SALAD NEEDS A TANGY DRESSING TO SUCCEED. THE
GARLIC AND LEMON-BASED DRESSING PROVIDES A TASTY
COMPLEMENT TO THE TEXTURE OF THE SALAD.

1 Boil the green beans in a pan of boiling water for 3 to 4 minutes and drain. Rinse the
beans well.

2 Put all the beans and the shallot in a bowl, sprinkle with salt and pepper, and mix well.

3 Combine the garlic, lemon juice, oil, and parsley in a jar, and shake well.

4 Lay the sliced tomatoes on a serving plate, pile the beans mixture in the center, sprinkle
with dressing, and garnish with olives.

nutrition facts	
energy	265 cal
	1105 kJ
protein	13 g
fat	15 g
of which saturated	2 g
carbohydrate	20 g
fiber	9 g
cholesterol	0 mg
sodium	370 mg

simmered **deep-fried egg** pouches

1 deep-fried beancurd pouch

1½ cups Japanese fish or vegan
  broth

4 tsp sugar

3 Tbsp Japanese soy sauce

3 Tbsp Japanese rice wine

4 small eggs

1 scallion, chopped

4 broccoli florets

THESE MAKE A GREAT APPETIZER. YOUR FRIENDS WILL HAVE NO IDEA
WHAT THEY HAVE BEFORE THEM! YOU CAN VARY THE FILLING, AND
MIX UP AN HERB AND SOY CHEESE OMELET INSTEAD OF USING THE
EGGS, FOR AN INTERESTING VARIATION.

1 Place the deep-fried beancurd pouch on a chopping board. Lightly roll with a rolling
pin, which makes it easier to open. Place the pouch in a sieve and rinse with hot water to
take off any excess oil. Cut the pouch in half and open pouch gently.

2 Put the broth, sugar, soy sauce, and rice wine in a pan and bring to a boil. Break the
eggs into the pouch, add the chopped scallion, and skewer the top of the pouch with a
cocktail stick to seal.

3 Put the pouch in a pan and simmer for 10 minutes.
Then add the broccoli to the pan and simmer for another
3 to 4 minutes. Serve hot.

nutrition facts	
energy	300 cal
	1248 kJ
protein	22 g
fat	20 g
of which saturated	5 g
carbohydrate	4 g
fiber	2 g
cholesterol	470 mg
sodium	1620 mg

minty **COUSCOUS** and soy sausage salad

SERVES 4

A MODERN, HEALTHY INTERPRETATION OF A LEVANTINE FAVORITE.

1 Tbsp extra-virgin olive oil

6 soy breakfast sausage links

1½ cups couscous

½ green bell pepper, seeded and chopped

4 Tbsp chopped fresh mint

4 Tbsp chopped fresh parsley

½ cup extra-virgin olive oil

5 lemons, squeezed

Salt and black pepper

1 medium tomato, chopped

Mint leaves and olives, for garnish

1 Heat the oil in a skillet and brown the sausage links lightly. Slice into ½-in-thick pieces.

2 Add the couscous to a pan containing twice the volume of water. Leave to swell for 5 minutes before draining.

3 Put the couscous, the sliced sausages, chopped pepper, mint, and parsley in a bowl and stir in the oil and lemon juice. Season with salt and pepper.

4 Serve the couscous in a bowl or on a plate, add the chopped tomato, and garnish with the mint leaves and olives to serve.

nutrition facts	
energy	470 cal
	1960 kJ
protein	17 g
fat	23 g
of which saturated	4 g
carbohydrate	37 g
fiber	1.5 g
cholesterol	1 mg
sodium	903 mg

arugula, **surimi stick**, and avocado salad with soy dressing

SERVES 4

IF YOU LIKE TO EAT SALADS EVERY DAY, AS I DO, YOU MAY SOMETIMES FIND OIL-BASED DRESSINGS A LITTLE TOO HEAVY FOR DAILY USE. THIS DRESSING USES NO OIL, GIVING A LIGHTER, FRESHER RESULT THAT ACCENTUATES THE TASTES AND TEXTURES OF THE SALAD.

1 bunch arugula, rinsed

10 surimi sticks, torn into strips

2 celery ribs, cut into long matchsticks

1 large avocado, pitted and chopped

2 medium cooked beets, cut into matchsticks

FOR THE DRESSING:

4 Tbsp Japanese soy sauce

1 Tbsp brown sugar

1 Tbsp freshly squeezed lemon juice

2 Tbsp sushi vinegar

2 Tbsp Japanese fish or vegan broth

1 Put the arugula, surimi strips, and celery in a salad bowl, and mix together. Add the avocado and beets.

2 In a jar, mix all the ingredients for the dressing and shake well until the sugar is dissolved. Sprinkle some dressing over the salad and serve.

nutrition facts	
energy	170 cal
	699 kJ
protein	9 g
fat	10 g
of which saturated	2 g
carbohydrate	12 g
fiber	2 g
cholesterol	22 mg
sodium	1302 mg

tempeh and **vegetable salad** with peanut dressing

SERVES 4

Oil for shallow frying

1½ cups tempeh, cut into bite-size pieces

1 cup baby corn, cut into halves

1 cup carrot, peeled and shredded

1 zucchini, shredded

1 cup bean sprouts, rinsed

1 green bell pepper, seeded and sliced

FOR THE PEANUT DRESSING:
(MAKES 1¼ CUPS)

6 Tbsp peanut butter

2 Tbsp light soy sauce

3 Tbsp sugar

3 Tbsp freshly squeezed lemon juice

½ cup water

¼ tsp ground chili powder

Butter lettuce and sliced tomatoes, for garnish

THE SECRET OF THIS RECIPE IS TO COOK THE VEGETABLES UNTIL THEY ARE STILL CRISP RATHER THAN TOO SOFT.

1 Heat the oil in a skillet. Shallow fry the tempeh until golden brown. Drain on paper towels.

2 Boil the baby corn, carrots, zucchini, and bean sprouts in a pan of boiling water for 3 to 4 minutes. Add the bell pepper for the final minute. Drain well.

3 Mix the peanut butter, soy sauce, sugar, lemon juice, water, and chili powder together and shake well in a jar.

4 Place the lettuce and sliced tomatoes on a serving plate and arrange the blanched vegetables and tempeh on the top. Drizzle the peanut dressing over the salad. Serve immediately.

nutrition facts	
energy	300 cal
	1246 kJ
protein	12 g
fat	15 g
of which saturated	2 g
carbohydrate	30 g
fiber	6 g
cholesterol	0 mg
sodium	542 mg

deep-fried **tempeh** with chili sauce

SERVES 4

1½ cups tempeh

Oil for deep-frying

2 butter lettuce leaves

1 tomato, sliced

1½-in cucumber, sliced

Chili sauce

CHILI SAUCE IS WIDELY AVAILABLE IN SUPERMARKETS AND SOUTH ASIAN FOOD STORES. IT IS MOSTLY USED WITH THAI CRISP SPRING ROLLS AND HAS A SWEET, PIQUANT FLAVOR. FOR THOSE WHO PREFER NOT TO USE CHOPSTICKS, IT MAY BE BETTER TO DRIZZLE THE CHILI SAUCE OVER THE DISH RATHER THAN HAVE IT IN A SEPARATE DISH FOR DIPPING.

1 Cut the tempeh in half, then slice into ½-inch pieces. Heat the oil to 325°F.

2 Deep-fry the tempeh for about 5 minutes or until golden brown. Drain well on paper towels. Place the tempeh on a bed of lettuce and garnish with the sliced tomato and cucumber, with the chili sauce in a small dish.

nutrition facts	
energy	180 cal
	744 kJ
protein	8 g
fat	15 g
of which saturated	2 g
carbohydrate	4 g
fiber	4 g
cholesterol	0 mg
sodium	4 mg

RIGHT tempeh and vegetable salad with peanut dressing

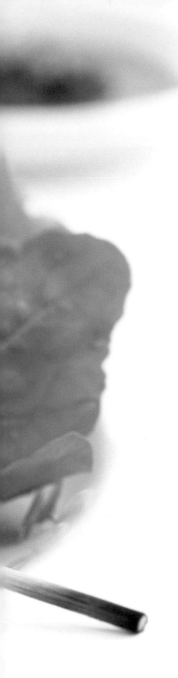

tofu and **tomato** **kabobs** with arugula

THIS DISH IS EQUALLY DELICIOUS MADE ON A BARBECUE AND SERVED ALFRESCO. FOR AN ALTERNATIVE, SERVE IN FRENCH BAGUETTES OR PITA BREADS.

MAKES 8 SKEWERS

2 zucchini, cut into 24 strips

11 oz firm tofu, cut into ½-in cubes (16)

24 cherry tomatoes

Extra-virgin olive oil

Salt and black pepper

1 Tbsp chopped fresh rosemary

1 Tbsp chopped fresh parsley

2 bunches arugula leaves, rinsed

FOR THE DRESSING:

2 tsp whole-grain mustard

3 Tbsp extra-virgin olive oil

2 Tbsp balsamic vinegar

2 tsp apple juice

1 Trim the zucchini strips. Wrap the tofu cubes with the strips, then slide the tomatoes and wrapped tofu pieces alternately onto the skewers to fill the length.

2 Brush with the olive oil and sprinkle with salt, black pepper, rosemary, and parsley. Broil the kabobs for 8 minutes, turning occasionally.

3 Mix the mustard, oil, balsamic vinegar, and apple juice in a jar and shake well.

4 Lay the arugula on a plate and place the kabobs on top, then drizzle with dressing.

nutrition facts	
energy	100 cal
	400 kJ
protein	4 g
fat	7.5 g
of which saturated	1 g
carbohydrate	3 g
fiber	1 g
cholesterol	0 mg
sodium	9 mg

soy sausage, pineapple, and rice salad

SERVES 4

1¾ cups long-grain rice

1 Tbsp sunflower oil

1 clove garlic, finely chopped

1 shallot, chopped fine

8 soy breakfast sausage links

½ red bell pepper, seeded and diced

1¼ cups canned pineapple, diced

Fresh basil leaves, for garnish

FOR THE DRESSING:

2 tsp whole-grain mustard

1 Tbsp canned pineapple juice

4 Tbsp sunflower oil

1 Tbsp white wine vinegar

Salt and black pepper

A MODERN SALAD WITH TASTY SOY SAUSAGES TO CONVERT EVEN THE MOST HARDENED SOY SCEPTIC.

1 Cook the rice according to page 14. Heat the oil in a skillet, add the garlic, shallot, and sausages, and sauté for 4 to 5 minutes.

2 Mix the mustard, pineapple juice, oil, vinegar, salt, and pepper in a jar and shake well.

3 Combine the cooked rice, sausage, bell pepper, and pineapple in a bowl. Stir in the dressing, and mix well. Serve, garnished with the basil leaves.

nutrition facts	
energy	655 cal
	2732 kJ
protein	21 g
fat	22 g
of which saturated	2.5 g
carbohydrate	93 g
fiber	2 g
cholesterol	1 mg
sodium	900 mg

potato and soy sausage salad

SERVES 4

20 baby potatoes, washed and cut into halves

1 Tbsp olive oil

4 soy breakfast sausage links, sliced

1 small red onion, sliced

10 cherry tomatoes, cut into halves

1 green bell pepper, seeded and diced

15 black olives, seeded and cut into halves

Salt and black pepper

FOR THE DRESSING:

2 Tbsp whole-grain mustard

6 Tbsp extra-virgin olive oil

2 Tbsp balsamic vinegar

2 tsp honey

SOY WIENERS AND BREAKFAST LINKS ARE SPICY, COMPLEX CREATIONS THAT I THINK ARE A GREAT ADDITION TO THE SAUSAGE FAMILY. THEY ARE A LITTLE FRAGILE AND SHOULD ONLY BE SLICED AFTER COOKING.

1 Put the water and potatoes in a pan, bring to a boil, and cook for about 10 minutes.

2 Meanwhile, heat the olive oil in a skillet, and sauté the wieners for 4 to 5 minutes. Rinse and soak the sliced onion in water until you are ready to use it.

3 Put the potatoes, wieners, onion, tomatoes, bell pepper, and olives in a bowl and generously sprinkle with salt and pepper.

4 In a jar, mix the mustard, oil, vinegar, and honey. Pour the dressing into the bowl and mix well with the other ingredients. Serve.

nutrition facts	
energy	390 cal
	1620 kJ
protein	11 g
fat	25 g
of which saturated	4 g
carbohydrate	32 g
fiber	4.5 g
cholesterol	0 mg
sodium	655 mg

egg rolls with tofu and vegetables

MAKES 8 ROLLS

1 Tbsp sunflower oil

1 tsp chopped fresh ginger

1 clove garlic, finely chopped

1 scallion, chopped

1 cup shiitake mushrooms, sliced thin

½ cup canned bamboo shoots, sliced thin

½ cup bean sprouts, rinsed

9 oz firm tofu, cut into strips

1 Tbsp light soy sauce

1 tsp sesame oil

1 tsp shaoxing rice wine (Chinese rice wine) or dry sherry

1 tsp sugar

1 tsp cornstarch

2 tsp water

8 egg roll sheets (8 x 8 in)

Oil for deep-frying

Soy sauce or chili sauce for dipping

A CLASSIC CHINESE DISH—THIS RECIPE MAKES ROLLS BIG ENOUGH TO BE EATEN AS A MAIN COURSE.

1 Heat the oil in a skillet, add the fresh ginger, garlic, and stir-fry for 1 minute. Add the scallion, mushrooms, bamboo shoots, and bean sprouts, then fry for 3 to 4 minutes.

2 Add the tofu, soy sauce, sesame oil, rice wine, and sugar, and fry for 2 more minutes. Dissolve the cornstarch into 2 teaspoons of water and stir in the mixture.

3 Fold each egg roll sheet into a diamond shape and then place 2 tablespoons of the filling on the lower side of the sheet. Roll the sheet up once and then fold each side into the center. Brush the water over the sheet so the corners stay in position. Repeat with the other sheets.

4 Heat the oil to 325°F and deep fry the rolls for a few minutes until lightly browned. Drain off excess oil and serve at once with soy sauce or chili sauce for dipping.

nutrition facts	
energy	80 cal
	350 kJ
protein	4.5 g
fat	3.5 g
of which saturated	0.5 g
carbohydrate	8.5 g
fiber	1 g
cholesterol	0 mg
sodium	111 mg

classic tofu and sweet miso sauce

SERVES 4

1 lb 2 oz tofu, cut into 1-in cubes

3 Tbsp white miso

1½ Tbsp mirin

3 Tbsp sugar

4 Tbsp Japanese fish or vegan broth

1 scallion, sliced diagonally

A TRADITIONAL JAPANESE DISH, THE STRONG FLAVOR OF THE SAUCE MEANS THAT THERE IS NO NEED TO MARINATE THE TOFU BEFOREHAND. THIS DISH IS MOST OFTEN MADE USING WHITE MISO BUT A DARK MISO REALLY DOES JUST AS WELL.

1 Put the tofu and water in a pan, and bring to a boil for about 4 minutes, and then drain. Meanwhile, put the miso, mirin, sugar, and broth into another pan, and bring to a boil. Simmer for 1 minute, stirring all the time.

2 Place the tofu on a plate, pour the miso sauce on it, and sprinkle with the sliced scallion. Serve hot or cold.

nutrition facts	
energy	170 cal
	700 kJ
protein	15 g
fat	6 g
of which saturated	0.6 g
carbohydrate	15 g
fiber	0 g
cholesterol	0 mg
sodium	494 mg

deep-fried **tofu** with vegetable julienne

SERVES 4

1 lb 2 oz firm tofu

All-purpose flour for coating

Oil for deep-frying

2 Tbsp carrot, shredded

3 Tbsp green bell pepper, shredded

2 Tbsp onion, shredded

2 Tbsp Japanese fish or vegan broth

2 Tbsp Japanese soy sauce

1 Tbsp mirin

1 tsp sugar

A pinch of salt

Cress or chopped watercress, for garnishing

THIS LIGHT AND DELICIOUS APPETIZER IS SUFFUSED WITH THE FLAVORS OF THE VEGETABLES.

1 Drain the excess water from the tofu on a cloth for about 3 minutes. Cut the tofu into 1½-in squares and coat with flour.

2 Heat the oil at 325°F in a pan and deep-fry the tofu until it has turned golden. Drain the excess oil onto paper towels.

3 Put the carrot, bell pepper, onion, and broth in a pan. Bring to a boil and simmer for 3 minutes.

4 Add the soy sauce, mirin, sugar, and a pinch of salt. Simmer for 3 more minutes.

5 Place the tofu in a separate dish. Pour over the sauce, garnish with cress, and serve while hot.

nutrition facts	
energy	280 cal
	1150 kJ
protein	11 g
fat	22 g
of which saturated	2.5 g
carbohydrate	8 g
fiber	0.5 g
cholesterol	0 mg
sodium	440 mg

deep-fried **won ton** with tempeh

SERVES 4

2 cloves garlic, finely chopped

½-in piece fresh ginger, finely chopped

4 scallions, chopped

1 cup canned bamboo shoots, chopped

1 cup tempeh, chopped

1 carrot, cut into short matchsticks

1 tsp sesame oil

1 tsp sugar

Salt and black pepper

12 fresh won ton wrappers

Oil for deep-frying

FOR THE DIPPING SAUCE:

1¼ cups water

4 Tbsp ketchup

4 Tbsp sugar

1 Tbsp Chinese light soy sauce

2 Tbsp malt vinegar

5 tsp cornstarch

TEMPEH IS AN INDONESIAN INVENTION—A MARVELOUS NUT-FLAVORED BLOCK OF FERMENTED SOYBEANS THAT IS LIKED BY EVERYONE WHO TRIES IT. THIS DISH COMBINES TEMPEH WITH A TYPICAL CHINESE DISH, FRIED WON TON.

1 Mix the garlic, ginger, scallion, bamboo shoots, tempeh, carrot, sesame oil, and sugar well in a bowl, and sprinkle generously with the salt and black pepper.

2 Put 1 tablespoon of the mixture onto the center of a won ton wrapper. Brush around the edges with water, and fold both sides in to create an envelope. Seal the center and edges. Alternatively, gather all the edges together to make a parcel.

3 Heat the oil in a pan to around 350°F. Deep-fry the won ton for a few minutes or until golden brown. Remove and drain on paper towels. If the oil gets too hot, the won ton wrappers will brown too quickly leaving the filling uncooked. To take the temperature down, adjust the heat or add a little more oil.

4 To make the dipping sauce, put all the ingredients into a pan. Stirring constantly, bring to a boil and then leave to simmer until the sauce thickens. Serve hot.

nutrition facts	
energy	460 cal
	1931 kJ
protein	13 g
fat	16 g
of which saturated	2 g
carbohydrate	66 g
fiber	5 g
cholesterol	0 mg
sodium	395 mg

RIGHT deep fried tofu with vegetable julienne

tomato and **olive** tart

A CLASSIC FRENCH TART RECIPE WITH A SOY PASTRY BASE.

SERVES 6

2 cups short crust pastry

2 Tbsp extra-virgin olive oil

2 cloves garlic, finely chopped

1 onion, sliced into rings

2 celery ribs, sliced thin

1 Tbsp fresh oregano
    (or 1 tsp dried)

Salt and black pepper

$\frac{1}{3}$ cup white wine

8 cherry tomatoes, cut into
    halves

10 black olives, pitted

Basil leaves, for garnish

1 Heat the oven 340°F. Make the short crust pastry according to the method on page 15. Roll out the pastry on a floured surface and line a pie pan. Cover with parchment paper, fill with pie weights, and bake for 10 minutes.

2 Heat the oil in a skillet, add the garlic, onion, and celery, and sauté for 3 minutes. Add the oregano, salt, pepper, and wine, and sauté for about 10 minutes or until the liquid has almost disappeared.

3 Preheat the oven to 350°F. Put the onion mixture into the pastry, and put the tomatoes and olives on the mixture. Bake in the oven for 35 to 40 minutes or until the filling is solid throughout.

nutrition facts	
energy	250 cal
	1036 kJ
protein	3 g
fat	18 g
of which saturated	5 g
carbohydrate	22 g
fiber	1.5 g
cholesterol	15 mg
sodium	291 mg

shrimp, roasted bell pepper, and green beans with soy and sesame dressing

SERVES 4

1 Tbsp sunflower oil

1 red bell pepper, halved and seeded

1 green bell pepper, halved and seeded

1 cup green beans, cut into halves

1 cup lettuce

9 oz shrimp

6 surimi sticks, sliced diagonally

Cilantro leaves

FOR THE SOY AND SESAME DRESSING:

2 Tbsp Japanese soy sauce

2 Tbsp sesame oil

2 Tbsp sunflower oil

½ clove garlic, finely chopped

2 tsp English mustard

1 Tbsp toasted sesame seeds

2 Tbsp sushi vinegar

SOY SAUCE DRESSINGS ARE NOW AVAILABLE READY-MADE IN MANY SUPERMARKETS BUT I HAVE YET TO FIND ANY THAT ARE AS GOOD AS A HOMEMADE DRESSING!

1 Brush the oil over the bell peppers, lay them on a greased baking sheet, put under the broiler and broil them until blackened. Peel the scorched skin off and slice the peppers.

2 Boil the green beans in a pan of boiling water for 3 to 4 minutes, and drain.

3 Combine the peppers, green beans, lettuce, half of the shrimp, and surimi slices in a salad bowl. Put the rest of shrimp on top and garnish with the cilantro.

4 Mix the soy sauce, sesame oil, sunflower oil, garlic, mustard, sesame seeds, and vinegar in a jar, and shake well. Pour the dressing over the salad just before serving.

nutrition facts	
energy	270 cal
	1109 kJ
protein	18 g
fat	17 g
of which saturated	2.5 g
carbohydrate	11 g
fiber	2.5 g
cholesterol	139 mg
sodium	745 mg

creamy crab and corn croquettes

MAKES 8 CROQUETTES

2 Tbsp soy margarine

½ medium onion, chopped

¼ cup all-purpose flour

½ cup soy milk

⅓ cup canned corn kernels

Two 4-oz cans, dressed crab

All-purpose flour, for coating

1 egg, beaten

Breadcrumbs, for coating

Oil for deep-frying

A RECIPE THAT IS WORTH THE EFFORT. THESE CROQUETTES ARE EXTREMELY VERSATILE AND PERFECT FOR ANYTHING FROM HORS D'OEUVRES TO PICNICS—A BIG FAVORITE WITH CHILDREN.

1 Melt the margarine in a pan, add the onion, and sauté for 3 to 4 minutes.

2 Add the flour, stirring well, then gradually pour the milk in, a little at a time, to thicken the sauce. Turn off the heat.

3 Add the corn and crab, and mix well. Let the mixture chill in the refrigerator for 30 minutes.

4 Divide the mixture into eight, and form into croquette shapes. Coat the eight croquettes in the following order: flour, egg, breadcrumbs. Leave them to stand again for 15 minutes.

5 Heat the oil to 325°F. Deep-fry the croquettes until golden brown. Remove from the pan and drain on paper towels before serving.

nutrition facts	
energy	230 cal
	950 kJ
protein	6 g
fat	16 g
of which saturated	2 g
carbohydrate	16 g
fiber	1 g
cholesterol	37 mg
sodium	175 mg

surimi sticks and scallion rafts with a lemon and miso sauce

SERVES 4

3 bunches scallions

15 surimi sticks

FOR THE LEMON AND MISO SAUCE:

5 Tbsp white miso

5 Tbsp mirin

5 tsp sugar

½ tsp lemon zest

½ tsp freshly squeezed lemon juice

SIMPLE INGREDIENTS COMBINE TO PRODUCE A REALLY GREAT FLAVOR FOR THIS DISH, WHICH CAN EITHER BE SERVED AS AN APPETIZER, OR AS A MAIN COURSE SERVED WITH RICE AND TWO EXTRA SURIMI STICKS ON EACH "RAFT."

1 Cut the scallions to the same length as the surimi sticks. Boil the scallions in a pan of water for 3 minutes. Drain, rinse with cold water, then squeeze off any excess watter.

2 To make the sauce, put the miso, mirin, and sugar in a pan over a low heat. Keep stirring for 1 to 2 minutes until the mixture is blended. Turn off the heat, add the lemon zest and juice, and mix well.

3 Place two surimi sticks on a plate, then lay the scallions crosswise. Repeat to create another layer of surimi sticks and another layer of scallions to form the small "raft." Pour the lemon and miso sauce over each raft, and serve.

nutrition facts	
energy	160 cal
	670 kJ
protein	11 g
fat	1.5 g
of which saturated	0 g
carbohydrate	23 g
fiber	1 g
cholesterol	29 mg
sodium	1221 mg

3 main dishes

Here you will find every soy product imaginatively combined with traditional ingredients in classic dishes from around the world. From laksa to lasagne you will find a range of tempting dishes that are easy to prepare and can be tailored to suit every occasion. Many dishes combine soy with meat, but these can be made to please the staunchest vegetarian with the simple substitution of more soy.

LEFT laksa lemak with tofu (page 82)

stir-fried **egg noodles** with tofu, red bell pepper, and **sugar snap** peas

SERVES 4

2½ cups medium egg noodles

1 Tbsp sesame oil

½ cup sugar snap peas, cut into halves

1 Tbsp sunflower oil

1 clove garlic, finely chopped

1-in piece of fresh ginger, finely chopped

6 scallions, sliced diagonally

1 red bell pepper, seeded and sliced

6 canned water chestnuts, sliced

½ cup bok choy, chopped

10 oz firm tofu, diced into ½-in cubes

1 Tbsp oyster sauce

3 Tbsp Chinese light soy sauce

1 tsp sugar

NOODLES ARE AS UBIQUITOUS IN ASIAN COOKERY AS TOFU. NO BOOK ABOUT ONE OF THESE WOULD BE COMPLETE WITHOUT A RECIPE THAT INCLUDED THE OTHER.

1 Cook the egg noodles in a pan of boiling water for 4 minutes. Drain and sprinkle 1 tablespoon of sesame oil over the noodles. Blanch the sugar snap peas in another pan of boiling water for 2 minutes, and drain.

2 Heat the sunflower oil in a wok or skillet, and stir-fry the garlic and ginger for 1 minute.

3 Add the scallions, red pepper, water chestnuts, and bok choy, and stir-fry for 2 to 3 minutes.

4 Add the tofu and stir-fry for 2 minutes. Add the oyster sauce, soy sauce, and sugar, and stir-fry for 2 minutes more. Serve hot.

nutrition facts	
energy	430 cal
	1806 kJ
protein	17 g
fat	14 g
of which saturated	3 g
carbohydrate	61 g
fiber	4 g
cholesterol	2 mg
sodium	938 mg

vietnamese-style **fried tofu** in tomato sauce

SERVES 4

1¼ cups broccoli florets

4 Tbsp soy or sunflower oil

14 oz firm tofu, cut into ½-in-thick bite-size pieces

FOR THE TOMATO SAUCE:

1 clove garlic, finely chopped

1 shallot, finely chopped

1 small red chile, chopped

14-oz can tomatoes

2 Tbsp fish sauce

2 tsp sugar

1 Tbsp fresh cilantro, chopped

1 Tbsp fresh mint leaves, chopped

Sliced cucumber, to garnish

A NONSTICK PAN IS REALLY USEFUL TO SAUTÉ THE TOFU WITHOUT IT STICKING OR BREAKING UP. IF YOU DON'T HAVE A NONSTICK PAN AVAILABLE, MAKE SURE YOUR SKILLET OR WOK IS VERY HOT BEFORE YOU BEGIN SAUTÉING THE TOFU.

1 Boil the broccoli in a pan of hot water for 3 minutes and drain. Heat 3 tablespoons of the oil in a skillet and sauté the tofu, browning it on both sides.

2 Heat the the remaining oil in a pan, stir-fry the garlic, shallot, and chile for 2 minutes. Add the tomatoes, fish sauce, and sugar, and simmer for about 15 minutes. Add the broccoli, tofu, cilantro, and mint.

3 Place the tofu on a serving plate, garnish with sliced cucumber, and serve.

nutrition facts	
energy	220 cal
	1910 kJ
protein	11 g
fat	16 g
of which saturated	2 g
carbohydrate	9 g
fiber	2 g
cholesterol	0 mg
sodium	358 mg

thai tofu **red curry**

Salt

½ eggplant, chopped

1 Tbsp sunflower oil

1 clove garlic, finely chopped

1 shallot, sliced

12 oz firm tofu, diced into
   1-in cubes

½ cup canned bamboo shoots

2 Tbsp Thai red curry paste

1¾ cups coconut milk

2 Tbsp fish sauce

1 tsp brown sugar

1 kaffir lime leaf

1 tsp freshly squeezed lime juice

1 Tbsp cilantro leaves, for
   garnish

ANOTHER ASIAN STAPLE—THIS TIME A DELICIOUS FUSION OF TASTES FOR WHICH THAILAND IS RIGHTLY FAMOUS. THAI RED CURRY PASTE IS NOW AVAILABLE FROM A WIDE RANGE OF SUPERMARKETS.

1 Sprinkle the salt over the eggplant pieces and leave for 15 to 20 minutes before lightly rinsing. Heat the oil in a pan and sauté the garlic and shallot for 1 minute.

2 Add the tofu, bamboo shoots, and Thai red curry paste, and stir-fry for 1 minute. Then add the coconut milk, fish sauce, brown sugar, lime leaf, and lime juice. Bring to a boil and simmer for 15 to 20 minutes.

3 Garnish with cilantro and serve with Thai fragrant rice.

nutrition facts	
energy	352 cal
	1471 kJ
protein	8 g
fat	28 g
of which saturated	17 g
carbohydrate	6 g
fiber	1.5 g
cholesterol	10 mg
sodium	432 mg

spinach and **soy** curry

4 Tbsp soy or sunflower oil

4 cloves garlic, finely chopped

1-in piece ginger, finely chopped

1 large onion, sliced

1 red chile, chopped

1 cup soy breakfast sausage
   links, finely chopped

1 cup red lentils, rinsed

2 tomatoes, peeled and chopped

1 tsp ground turmeric

1 Tbsp ground cumin

1 green cardamom, lightly
   crushed

¼ tsp fenugreek seeds

1 tsp garam masala

1 tsp salt

2 cloves

4 cups water

1 potato, peeled and coarsely
   diced

FINELY CHOPPED SOY SAUSAGE LINKS RETAIN THEIR TEXTURE WELL, NO MATTER WHICH WAY IT IS COOKED, AND EASILY ABSORBS THE FLAVORS OF THIS SPICY DISH.

1 Heat the oil in a pan, add the garlic, ginger, onion, and chile, and stir-fry for 3 to 4 minutes. Add the minced soy sausage, lentils, and tomatoes, and stir-fry for 2 minutes.

2 Add the turmeric, cumin, cardamom, fenugreek, and garam masala, and stir-fry for 2 to 3 minutes. Add the salt, cloves, and water, bring to a boil, and simmer for 15 minutes.

3 Add the potato, spinach, sugar, ketchup, and lemon juice, and simmer for 10 to 15 minutes more. Serve hot with basmati rice and sprinkled with chopped cilantro.

2 cups fresh spinach

2 tsp sugar

4 Tbsp ketchup

2 Tbsp freshly squeezed lemon
   juice

Basmati rice and chopped fresh
   cilantro, to serve

nutrition facts	
energy	500 cal
	2104 kJ
protein	41 g
fat	13 g
of which saturated	1.5 g
carbohydrate	58 g
fiber	16 g
cholesterol	0 mg
sodium	699 mg

teriyaki **tofu**

A JAPANESE DISH, "TERIYAKI" MEANS LITERALLY "BROILED TO A SHINE." THE TERIYAKI METHOD CAN BE APPLIED TO MANY DIFFERENT FOODS RATHER THAN JUST TO TOFU. IN JAPAN, THE MOST COMMON ASSOCIATION IS WITH CHICKEN.

SERVES 4

1 lb 7oz firm tofu, diced into ½-in cubes

2 Tbsp sunflower oil

6 Tbsp Japanese soy sauce

4 Tbsp mirin

4 Tbsp sugar

Bean sprouts, for garnish

Chopped scallion, for garnish

1 Tbsp toasted sesame seeds

1 Drain the excess water from the tofu on a cloth for 3 to 4 minutes. Heat the oil in a skillet and lightly brown the tofu. Remove the tofu from the oil and drain on paper towels.

2 In the same pan, put the soy sauce, mirin, and sugar. Bring to a boil and simmer for a few minutes until the sauce has thickened.

3 Put the tofu cubes back into the pan and stir for 1 to 2 minutes. Garnish with the bean sprouts and scallion, then sprinkle with the sesame seeds and serve.

nutrition facts	
energy	272 cal
	1136 kJ
protein	15 g
fat	14 g
of which saturated	2 g
carbohydrate	19 g
fiber	0 g
cholesterol	0 mg
sodium	1295 mg

soy sausage, zucchini, and red bell pepper kabobs

THESE DELICIOUS KABOBS ARE IDEAL FOR A VEGETARIAN BARBECUE. THE SAUSAGES ARE READY TO EAT WHEN THE VEGETABLES ARE COOKED—SO THESE KABOBS ARE DELICIOUS AND QUICK AS THERE'S NO MEAT TO WAIT FOR!

MAKES 8 SKEWERS

- 1 red bell pepper, seeded and cut into large bite-size pieces
- 6 soy breakfast sausage links, cut into 1-in pieces
- 1 medium onion, cut into large bite-size pieces
- 6 medium zucchini, cut into 1-in pieces
- Salt and black pepper

FOR THE MARINADE:

- 1 orange, freshly squeezed
- ½ lemon, freshly squeezed
- 1 Tbsp honey
- 1 Tbsp chopped fresh cilantro

1 To make the marinade, mix the squeezed orange and lemon juices, honey, and cilantro well in a bowl.

2 In this order, put red pepper, sausage, onion, and zucchini pieces on a skewer and repeat this twice. Make seven more kabobs. Sprinkle with salt and black pepper.

3 In a large dish, marinate the kabobs in the orange-lemon mixture for at least 30 minutes.

4 Broil the kabobs, turning them occasionally. Put the remaining marinade in a small pan. Bring to a boil, then simmer for 2 to 3 minutes. Place the broiled kabobs on a plate and drizzle with the marinade.

nutrition facts	
energy	100 cal
	430 kJ
protein	8 g
fat	4 g
of which saturated	0.5 g
carbohydrate	8 g
fiber	2 g
cholesterol	0 mg
sodium	453 mg

fried **soy sausage links** and onion in sweet soy sauce

SERVES 4

1¾ cups long-grain rice, rinsed

1 Tbsp sunflower oil

1 medium onion, sliced

8 soy breakfast sausage links, sliced diagonally

1 green bell pepper, seeded and sliced

2 Tbsp mirin

3 Tbsp Japanese soy sauce

2 Tbsp sugar

1 Tbsp watercress, rinsed

TO MAKE A LIGHTER VERSION OF THIS RECIPE, SUBSTITUTE A GREEN LEAF AND TOMATO SALAD FOR THE RICE.

1 Cook the rice following the method on page 14.

2 Heat the oil in a skillet and sauté the onion, sausages, and pepper for 4 to 5 minutes.

3 Stir in the mirin, soy sauce, and sugar, and continue to sauté for 3 to 4 more minutes.

4 Place the rice in a serving bowl or on a plate and top with the sausage mixture. Garnish with the watercress and serve hot.

nutrition facts	
energy	630 cal
	2625 kJ
protein	26 g
fat	13 g
of which saturated	2 g
carbohydrate	98 g
fiber	2.5 g
cholesterol	1 mg
sodium	1847 mg

soy meatballs with fusilli

SERVES 4

4-oz package soy burgermix

1 small egg, beaten

½ cup water

3 Tbsp extra-virgin olive oil

1 clove garlic

1 celery rib, finely chopped

1 medium onion, chopped

14-oz can tomatoes

3 Tbsp red wine

1 Tbsp chopped fresh basil leaves

2 cups canned or frozen soybeans

Salt and black pepper

4 cups dried fusilli

Pinch of salt

THIS DELICIOUS PASTA DISH MAKES AN EXCELLENT WARMING MEAL. THE "MEATBALLS" BECOME INFUSED WITH THE RICH, GARLICKY TOMATO SAUCE.

1 Put the burgermix, egg, and water into a bowl, mix, and stand for 15 minutes. Meanwhile, heat the oil in a pan and sauté the garlic, celery, and onion for 3 to 4 minutes. Add the tomatoes, red wine, basil, and soybeans, and bring to a boil.

2 Form the soy mixture into small walnut shapes and put them into the tomato sauce. Simmer for 20 to 30 minutes, and season with salt and black pepper to taste.

3 Boil the fusilli in a pan of hot water with a pinch of salt for 8 to 10 minutes, or until *al dente* (firm to the bite). Drain well.

4 Serve the fusilli in bowls topped with the "meatballs" and hot tomato sauce.

nutrition facts	
energy	560 cal
	2332 kJ
protein	42 g
fat	35 g
of which saturated	6 g
carbohydrate	17 g
fiber	4 g
cholesterol	121 mg
sodium	213 mg

stir-fried tofu and cabbage

CABBAGE IS A VERY UNDERRATED VEGETABLE THAT PROBABLY HAS NEVER RECOVERED FROM ITS IMAGE AS BEING OVERBOILED AND UNAPPETIZING. PROPERLY PREPARED, IT IS DELICIOUS AND AN EXCELLENT SOURCE OF TRACE ELEMENTS AND DIETARY FIBER. USE NEW GREEN SOFT CABBAGE FOR STIR-FRY DISHES. IF YOU CANNOT FIND SHIITAKE MUSHROOMS, USE BUTTON MUSHROOMS INSTEAD. MAKE SURE THE PAN IS HOT WHEN YOU STIR-FRY THE TOFU, OR IT WILL STICK.

SERVES 4

5 Tbsp soy or sunflower oil

14 oz firm tofu, drained, cut in half, and sliced into ½-in pieces

1 medium cabbage (discard the stem part and cut leaves into large bite-size pieces)

1 medium onion, cut into large bite-size pieces

1 green bell pepper, seeded and cut into large bite-size pieces

1½ cups fresh shiitake mushrooms, cut into halves

4 Tbsp ketchup

1 Tbsp brown sauce

Salt and black pepper

Boiled rice, to serve

1 Heat 3 tablespoons of the oil in a skillet. Lightly brown the tofu on both sides, then remove and drain on paper towels. Clean the pan.

2 Heat the remaining oil in the skillet. Add the cabbage and onion, and stir-fry for 3 to 4 minutes. Add the bell pepper and mushrooms, and stir-fry for 2 to 3 minutes.

3 Add the tofu, ketchup, and brown sauce, and stir-fry for 3 to 4 minutes. Season with the salt and pepper to taste. Serve with rice.

nutrition facts	
energy	270 cal
	1110 kJ
protein	12 g
fat	19 g
of which saturated	2 g
carbohydrate	14 g
fiber	3 g
cholesterol	0 mg
sodium	217 mg

mushrooms, soy sausage links, and spinach spaghetti

SERVES 4

1lb spaghetti

4 Tbsp extra-virgin olive oil

4 cloves garlic, sliced

6 soy breakfast sausage links, sliced diagonally

1½ cups shiitake mushrooms, sliced

1½ cups oyster mushrooms, sliced

2 cups button mushrooms, sliced

2 cups fresh spinach

½ cup white wine

Salt and black pepper

4 Tbsp balsamic vinegar

1 Tbsp chopped fresh basil

THERE IS AN ALMOST INFINITE NUMBER OF PASTA COMBINATIONS. THIS RECIPE MAKES A LIGHT, HEALTHY MAIN COURSE, OR A STARTER USING HALF THE STATED INGREDIENT QUANTITIES.

1 Cook the spaghetti in a pan of boiling water until *al dente* (firm to the bite). Drain.

2 Heat the oil in a skillet, add the garlic, and sauté for 1 minute. Add the sausages, shiitake, oyster, and button mushrooms, and the spinach, and continue to sauté for 3 to 4 more minutes.

3 Add the wine and season with salt and pepper to taste. Continue to stir for about 3 minutes. Add the balsamic vinegar and basil, and stir for 1 minute more.

4 Add the spaghetti and combine well. Serve hot.

nutrition facts	
energy	655 cal
	2764 kJ
protein	29 g
fat	21 g
of which saturated	3 g
carbohydrate	88 g
fiber	6 g
cholesterol	1 mg
sodium	945 mg

soy mince lasagne

YELLOW LENTILS NEED TO BE SOAKED FOR AROUND 12 HOURS OR OVERNIGHT, THEN BOILED IN WATER FOR 10 MINUTES BEFORE USE.

SERVES 4

1 cup soy mince

1 onion

3 cloves garlic

1 celery rib

1 carrot

1 small eggplant

4 Tbsp extra-virgin olive oil

1 cup cooked yellow lentils

⅓ cup red wine

Two 14-oz cans tomatoes

4 Tbsp tomato paste

1 Tbsp chopped fresh oregano

2 Tbsp chopped fresh basil

2 Tbsp chopped fresh parsley

Salt and black pepper

10 lasagne sheets

FOR THE WHITE SAUCE:

2 Tbsp soy margarine

¼ cup all-purpose flour

1½ cups soy milk

Salt and black pepper

1 Preheat the oven to 350°F. Put the soy mince in a pan of hot water, cook for 2 to 3 minutes, then drain. Chop the onion, garlic, celery, carrot, and eggplant in a food processor.

2 Heat the oil in a pan, sauté the chopped vegetables, lentils, and soy mince for 3 to 4 minutes. Add the red wine, tomatoes, tomato paste, oregano, basil, and parsley, and cook for 20 to 30 minutes. Season with the salt and pepper.

3 Melt the margarine in a pan. Mix the flour into the margarine, stir well over a low heat, and gradually add the milk, a little at a time, mixing well to make a smooth sauce. Season with the salt and pepper.

4 Layer the sheets of lasagne and soy mince mixture alternately in an ovenproof dish, and finish with the white sauce. Bake in the oven for 30 minutes or until the top is lightly browned.

nutrition facts	
energy	540 cal
	2282 kJ
protein	28 g
fat	20 g
of which saturated	3 g
carbohydrate	61 g
fiber	11.5 g
cholesterol	0 mg
sodium	590 mg

baked peppers stuffed with soy sausage, **apricots**, and rice

SERVES 4

1 cup long-grain rice

1 Tbsp olive oil

2 cloves garlic, finely chopped

1 small onion, finely chopped

6 soy breakfast sausage links, cut into quarters lengthwise and chopped

10 dried apricots, chopped

2 Tbsp raisins

2 tsp mixed herbs

Salt and black pepper

3 red bell peppers (tops cut off but set aside), seeded

3 green bell peppers, as above

2 yellow bell peppers, as above

1¾ cups vegetable broth

A HEALTHY AND SATISFYING SUMMER DISH THAT IS EQUALLY GOOD SERVED HOT OR COLD.

1 Cook the rice according to page 14. Heat the oil in a skillet. Add the garlic, onion, and sausages, and sauté for 3 to 4 minutes. Preheat the oven 375°F.

2 Add the apricots, raisins, and mixed herbs, and sauté for 2 to 3 minutes. Add the cooked rice, stir, and season well with salt and pepper.

3 Fill the peppers with the rice mixture and place them in an ovenproof dish. Add the broth. Put the pepper tops on and bake for 30 to 40 minutes. Serve the peppers at once or leave to cool and serve cold.

nutrition facts	
energy	512 cal
	2145 kJ
protein	22 g
fat	11 g
of which saturated	0 g
carbohydrate	2 g
fiber	81 g
cholesterol	8 mg
sodium	1102 mg

baked red lentil and **zucchini** pie

SERVES 4

1½ cups whole-wheat flour

6 Tbsp soy margarine

Pinch of salt

1 Tbsp chopped fresh cilantro

2 to 3 Tbsp cold water

FOR THE FILLING:

1 Tbsp extra-virgin olive oil

1 clove garlic, finely chopped

1 onion, chopped

½ cup red lentils, rinsed

3 zucchini, sliced thin

⅔ cup frozen corn kernels

1½ cups vegetable broth

Salt and black pepper

Flour for dusting

Some milk for brushing

A SIMPLY PREPARED BUT NOURISHING AND HEALTHY VEGETARIAN OPTION FOR COLDER DAYS, THIS MAKES A FILLING LUNCH, OR A DINNER SERVED WITH A SELECTION OF OTHER VEGETABLES.

1 To make the short crust pastry, follow the recipe on page 15, adding the cilantro to the mixture as you mix it.

2 Heat the oil in a pan, add the garlic and onion, and sauté for 3 minutes. Add the lentils, zucchini, corn kernels, and broth. Bring to a boil and simmer for about 20 minutes or until the liquid is substantially reduced. Season with salt and pepper to taste.

3 Preheat the oven to 375°F. Place the lentil mixture in an ovenproof dish. Next, dust the top with the flour, roll out the pastry and cut out 2-in rounds with a small pastry cutter. Place the rounds of pastry on the mixture and brush with the milk. Bake for 20 to 25 minutes, or until lightly rowned.

nutrition facts	
energy	500 cal
	2074 kJ
protein	16 g
fat	22 g
of which saturated	4 g
carbohydrate	63 g
fiber	4 g
cholesterol	0 mg
sodium	576 mg

soybean **falafel**

FALAFEL ARE MORE TYPICALLY MADE FROM GARBANZO BEANS BUT SOYBEANS MAKE AN EQUALLY TASTY AND NUTRITIOUS SUBSTITUTE.

1 small onion

2 cloves garlic

2 slices bread

1 tsp ground cumin

1 tsp ground coriander

1 fresh red chile

½ tsp salt

1 Tbsp chopped fresh parsley

1 egg

2½ cups canned or frozen soybeans, drained

All-purpose flour, for coating

Oil for frying

1 Put the onion, garlic, bread, cumin, coriander, chile, salt, and parsley in a food mixer and process them coarsely.

2 Add the egg and soybeans, and process again until coarsely chopped.

3 Form the bean mixture into golf-ball sized balls, then lightly flatten to a patty shape and coat with flour.

4 Heat the oil in a skillet and shallow-fry the falafel until golden brown. Drain well on paper towels. Serve stuffed in pita bread with sliced tomatoes and lettuce.

nutrition facts	
energy	325 cal
	1360 kJ
protein	17 g
fat	20 g
of which saturated	3 g
carbohydrate	20 g
fiber	6 g
cholesterol	60 mg
sodium	153 mg

soybean **fajitas**

MAKES 8 FAJITAS

IF YOU PREFER A MILDER VERSION OF THESE FIERY FAJITAS, ADD ONLY ¼ TEASPOON OF CHILI POWDER.

2 Tbsp soy or sunflower oil

1 red onion, sliced

6 to 8 soy breakfast sausage links, sliced diagonally

1 red bell pepper, seeded and sliced

1 green bell pepper, seeded and sliced

2 cloves garlic, crushed

1 Heat the oil in a skillet, add the onion, sausages, bell peppers, and crushed garlic, and stir-fry for 4 to 5 minutes.

2 Add the cumin, coriander, lemon juice, chili powder, cinnamon, sugar, and oregano, and sprinkle with salt and pepper. Stir-fry for another 3 to 4 minutes. Stir in the cilantro.

3 Serve hot with tortillas, garnishing with lettuce and tomato, and the Spicy Avocado and Red Pepper Dip, if you like.

FOR THE SEASONING:

½ Tbsp ground cumin

½ Tbsp ground coriander

1 Tbsp freshly squeezed lemon juice

½ to 1 tsp chili powder

½ tsp ground cinnamon

1 tsp sugar

1 tsp dried oregano

Salt and black pepper

2 Tbsp fresh cilantro leaves

8 tortillas

Lettuce, sliced tomato, and Spicy Avocado and Red Pepper Dip (optional)—see page 109—to garnish

nutrition facts	
energy	220 cal
	921 kJ
protein	10 g
fat	7 g
of which saturated	1 g
carbohydrate	31 g
fiber	2.5 g
cholesterol	0 mg
sodium	546 mg

soy burger, broiled eggplant, and bell pepper towers with pesto sauce

BOTH CHILDREN AND ADULTS WILL ENJOY THESE. FOR THE YOUNGSTERS, YOU MIGHT THINK ABOUT SERVING THE BURGERS WITH THE EGGPLANT AND PEPPERS IN FRESH TOASTED BUNS. YOU CAN CHEAT AND USE A READY-MADE PESTO SAUCE IF YOU PREFER, BUT YOU MAY NEED TO ADD MORE OLIVE OIL TO REACH THE DESIRED CONSISTENCY.

SERVES 4

4-oz package soy burgermix

1 small egg, beaten

½ cup water

4 Tbsp extra-virgin olive oil

4 slices of eggplant

1 green bell pepper, seeded and cut into quarters

4 medium tomato slices

4 stalks fresh tarragon

FOR THE PESTO SAUCE:

¼ cup fresh basil leaves

1 clove garlic

1 Tbsp pine nuts

3 Tbsp extra-virgin olive oil

¼ tsp salt

Black pepper

1 Put the burgermix, egg, and water into a bowl. Leave to stand for 15 minutes or according to the instructions on the burgermix package. Form into 4 burger shapes.

2 Brush both sides of the burgers, eggplant, bell peppers, and tomatoes with olive oil and sauté in a griddle pan until lightly browned. Alternatively, you could use a skillet, heating the oil in the pan first.

3 Put the ingredients for the pesto sauce in a food processor, and blend to a purée.

4 Pile up the tomato, bell pepper, burger, and eggplant on a serving plate. Secure them with a stalk of tarragon, drizzle with the pesto sauce, and serve.

nutrition facts	
energy	350 cal
	1468 kJ
protein	13 g
fat	27 g
of which saturated	3 g
carbohydrate	15 g
fiber	1.5 g
cholesterol	60 mg
sodium	26 mg

soy **toad-in-the-hole**

SERVES 4

1 cup all-purpose flour

2 eggs, beaten

1¼ cups soy milk

Salt and black pepper

8 soy breakfast sausage links

1 Tbsp chopped fresh parsley

THE TRADITIONAL ENGLISH SUPPER DISH WITH A NOT-SO-TRADITIONAL SOY TWIST!

1 Sieve the flour into a bowl, add the beaten eggs, and mix well with a fork. Add the soy milk, sprinkle over the salt and pepper, then whisk very well. Let the mixture stand for 30 minutes. Preheat the oven to 375°F.

2 Place the sausages in an ovenproof dish and pour the batter in. Bake in the oven for about 30 minutes or until the batter is golden brown. Sprinkle with the chopped parsley and serve hot.

nutrition facts	
energy	350 cal
	1473 kJ
protein	26 g
fat	15 g
of which saturated	2.5 g
carbohydrate	30 g
fiber	2 g
cholesterol	118 mg
sodium	1266 mg

braised tofu, onion, and egg on rice

SERVES 4

1¾ cups Japanese short-grain rice

1 Tbsp sunflower oil

1 medium onion, sliced

1 cup Japanese fish or vegan broth (see page 13)

2 Tbsp Japanese soy sauce

2 Tbsp mirin

2 tsp sugar

1 lb 2 oz firm tofu, halved lengthwise and cut into ½-in slices

1 tsp bonito flakes

2 eggs, beaten

2 scallions, chopped

IT IS VERY COMMON IN JAPAN TO COMBINE BEATEN EGG WITH MEAT AND VEGETABLES OVER RICE OR NOODLES. THE MOST WELL-KNOWN COMBINATION IS "MOTHER AND CHILD," MEANING BEATEN EGG COMBINED WITH CHICKEN. THIS COMBINATION, USING TOFU, IS EVERY BIT AS NUTRITIOUS AND DERIVES ITS DELICIOUS FLAVOR FROM THE USE OF MIRIN AND SOY SAUCE.

1 Cook the rice according to the instructions on page 14. Heat the oil in a skillet, add the onion, and sauté it for 2 to 3 minutes.

2 Add the broth, soy sauce, mirin, and sugar. Bring to a boil, then add the tofu and simmer for 5 minutes.

3 Sprinkle in the bonito flakes and pour in the beaten eggs. Put a lid on the pan and simmer for about 2 minutes.

4 Place the rice in a bowl or on a plate, and top with tofu mixture. Garnish with the chopped scallions.

nutrition facts	
energy	560 cal
	2336 kJ
protein	23 g
fat	12 g
of which saturated	2 g
carbohydrate	86 g
fiber	0 g
cholesterol	125 mg
sodium	620 mg

penne with **soy sausage links** and **eggplant** in pimento sauce

SALTING THE EGGPLANT REDUCES ANY BITTERNESS. MAKE SURE YOU REMOVE THE EXCESS SALT BEFORE YOU COOK IT.

SERVES 4

1 large eggplant, cut into bite-size pieces

Salt

5 cups penne (dried)

2 Tbsp olive oil

6 soy breakfast sausage links, sliced

12 black olives, pitted and cut into halves

Basil leaves, for garnish

FOR THE PIMENTO SAUCE:

1 Tbsp olive oil

1 clove garlic, finely chopped

½ small onion, finely chopped

1 fresh red chile, finely chopped

14-oz can tomatoes, chopped

1 Tbsp chopped fresh basil leaves

Salt and black pepper

1 Sprinkle a little salt over the eggplant pieces and leave for 30 minutes. Rinse off excess salt with running water.

2 Meanwhile, heat the tablespoon of oil in a pan, then sauté the garlic, onion, and chile for 2 minutes. Add the tomato and basil. Season with salt and pepper, and simmer for 30 minutes.

3 Boil the penne in a pan of boiling water until *al dente* (firm to the bite). Drain well.

4 Heat the 2 tablespoons of oil in a skillet, sauté the eggplant and sausages for about 5 minutes. Add the sliced olives and the pimento sauce, and cook for 3 to 5 minutes.

5 Stir the penne into the sauce and serve garnished with the basil leaves.

nutrition facts	
energy	650 cal
	2738 kJ
protein	29 g
fat	19 g
of which saturated	3 g
carbohydrate	6 g
fiber	8 g
cholesterol	1 mg
sodium	1159 mg

red cabbage, apple, and soy sausage link casserole

A HEARTY EASTERN EUROPEAN WARMER, TAILORED TO SUIT A HEALTHIER LIFESTYLE.

SERVES 4

2 Tbsp olive oil

8 soy breakfast sausage links, cut into halves

2 cloves garlic, finely chopped

1 red onion, sliced

½ small red cabbage, shredded

1 apple, chopped

½ cup raisins

4 Tbsp red wine

4 Tbsp red wine vinegar

2 Tbsp sugar

1 clove

Salt and black pepper

1 Heat the oil in a pan. Sauté the sausages, garlic, and red onion for 3 to 4 minutes. Add the red cabbage and sauté for 4 more minutes. **2** Add the apple, raisins, red wine, vinegar, sugar, and clove. Generously sprinkle with salt and pepper. Simmer with the lid on for 30 to 40 minutes before serving with mashed potato made with soy butter or milk.

nutrition facts	
energy	360 cal
	1499 kJ
protein	19 g
fat	15 g
of which saturated	2 g
carbohydrate	34 g
fiber	4 g
cholesterol	1 mg
sodium	1218 mg

laksa lemak with **tofu**

SERVES 4

1½ cups rice vermicelli

½ cup sugar snap peas

½ cup bean sprouts

5 Tbsp sunflower oil

6 shallots, finely chopped

3 cloves garlic, finely chopped

1-in piece fresh ginger, finely chopped

3 fresh small green chiles, chopped

1 Tbsp chopped lemon grass

2 tsp ground turmeric

1 tsp ground coriander

2¼ cups chicken or vegetable broth

3½ cups coconut milk

2 tsp sugar

2 tsp salt

14 oz firm tofu

4 scallions, sliced diagonally

A MALAYSIAN SPECIALTY THAT BECOMES A FIRM FAVORITE WITH ALL WHO TRY IT.

1 Soak the vermicelli in hot water for 3 minutes, then rinse and drain. Blanch the peas and bean sprouts in a pan of boiling water for 2 minutes and drain.

2 Heat 3 tablespoons of the oil in a pan, add the shallots, garlic, ginger, chiles, lemon grass, turmeric, and coriander, and sauté for 3 minutes.

3 Add the broth, coconut milk, sugar, and salt. Bring to a boil and simmer for 3 minutes. Add the tofu and continue to simmer for another 3 minutes.

4 Put the rice vermicelli into individual bowls and pour in the soup. Put the bean sprouts, peas, and tofu on top of the noodles. Pour the soup over all, garnish with sliced scallions, and serve.

nutrition facts	
energy	917 cal
	3830 kJ
protein	14 g
fat	64 g
of which saturated	38 g
carbohydrate	46 g
fiber	2 g
cholesterol	0 mg
sodium	1167 mg

soy **chili con carne**

SERVES 4

4 Tbsp extra-virgin olive oil

3 cloves garlic, finely chopped

1 large onion, finely chopped

1 cup soy mince

3 cups button mushrooms, finely chopped

1 green bell pepper, seeded and finely chopped

1 red bell pepper, seeded and finely chopped

14-oz can tomatoes

14-oz can red kidney beans

1¾ cups water

3 Tbsp tomato paste

½ tsp chili powder

3 tsp ground cinnamon

3 tsp allspice

Salt

IF YOU HAVE EVER BEEN PUT OFF EATING A BEEF CHILI CON CARNE BECAUSE OF ITS OILINESS OR THE FILM OF FAT THAT FORMS ON THE LEFTOVERS, THEN THIS IS THE RECIPE FOR YOU. I CALL THIS A "BASELINE" RECIPE BECAUSE THE HEAT IS KEPT TO A MODERATE LEVEL, TO SUIT EVERYONE. IF YOU LIKE MORE HEAT, SIMPLY ADD MORE CHILI!

1 Heat the oil in a pan, add the garlic and onion, and sauté for 2 to 3 minutes. Add the soy mince, mushrooms, and bell peppers, and sauté for 3 to 4 minutes.

2 Add the canned tomatoes, red kidney beans, water, tomato paste, chili powder, cinnamon, and allspice, then bring to a boil and simmer for 30 minutes. Season with salt to taste. Serve hot with rice.

nutrition facts	
energy	440 cal
	1845 kJ
protein	26 g
fat	17 g
of which saturated	2 g
carbohydrate	47 g
fiber	10 g
cholesterol	0 mg
sodium	415 mg

tofu and **broccoli** in sweet and sour sauce

SERVES 4

1⅔ cups broccoli florets

1 carrot, thickly sliced

1 tsp sesame oil

2 tsp sunflower oil

1 clove garlic, finely chopped

½-in piece fresh ginger, finely chopped

1 medium onion, diced

11 oz firm tofu, diced into ½-in cubes

1½ cups shiitake mushrooms, thickly sliced

Salt and black pepper

FOR THE SAUCE:

1½ cups chicken or vegetable broth

1 Tbsp shaoxing wine (Chinese rice wine) or dry sherry

2 Tbsp sugar

3 Tbsp ketchup

2 Tbsp Chinese light soy sauce

2 Tbsp vinegar

1½ Tbsp cornstarch

3 Tbsp water

A TASTY AND EASILY PREPARED DISH THAT IS BEST EATEN WITH A BOWL OF STEAMING RICE.

1 Blanch the broccoli and carrot in a pan of boiling water for 3 minutes before draining.

2 Heat the sesame and sunflower oils in a wok or skillet, add the garlic, ginger, and onion, and stir-fry for 2 to 3 minutes. Add the tofu and stir-fry for another 2 to 3 minutes.

3 Add the broccoli, carrot, and mushrooms before stir-frying for 2 more minutes. Sprinkle with a pinch of salt and pepper. Add the broth, rice wine, sugar, ketchup, soy sauce, and vinegar and bring to a boil. Simmer for 2 to 3 minutes.

4 Dissolve the cornstarch with water and stir into the pan to thicken the sauce. Serve hot.

nutrition facts	
energy	190 cal
	790 kJ
protein	11 g
fat	6 g
of which saturated	1 g
carbohydrate	22 g
fiber	3 g
cholesterol	0 mg
sodium	754 mg

salmon and leek
fish pie with fluffy potato

A VARIATION ON THE TRADITIONAL FISHERMAN'S PIE WITH SOY
SUBSTITUTES FOR THE DAIRY CONSTITUENTS.

SERVES 4

3 large potatoes, peeled
1 lb fresh salmon steaks
⅓ cup soy milk
¾ cup vegetable broth
¼ cup soy margarine
1 small leek, sliced
⅓ cup all-purpose flour
1 tsp English mustard
1 Tbsp chopped fresh parsley
Salt and black pepper

1 Put the potatoes and water in a pan and slowly bring to a boil. When the liquid reaches boiling point, turn off the heat and drain.

2 Put the salmon, milk, and broth in another pan, bring to a boil, and simmer for 10 minutes. Take the salmon out and break up into flakes. Retain the liquid and let it cool.

3 Melt the margarine in a skillet and sauté the leek until softened. Add the flour and stir for 1 minute. Stir in the liquid little by little to incorporate it evenly into the flour mixture. Preheat the oven to 400°F.

4 Add the mustard and parsley, and mix well. Then add the flaked salmon and season with salt and pepper.

5 Grate the potatoes. Put the salmon mixture into an ovenproof dish and top with the grated potatoes. Bake in the oven for 20 minutes or until golden brown.

nutrition facts	
energy	470 cal
	1958 kJ
protein	30 g
fat	22 g
of which saturated	4 g
carbohydrate	39 g
fiber	4 g
cholesterol	56 mg
sodium	216 mg

cod with creamed mushroom sauce

THE ADDITION OF SOY CREAM RATHER THAN DAIRY CREAM TO
THIS RECIPE HELPS TO REDUCE THE FAT IN THIS POPULAR
CLASSIC DISH.

SERVES 4

4 cod fillets

Salt and black pepper

1 clove garlic, finely chopped

**1½ cups button mushrooms,
chopped**

1 Tbsp chopped fresh parsley

1 cup soy cream

1 Preheat the oven to 350°F. Place the cod
fillets in an ovenproof dish and generously
sprinkle with salt and pepper. Arrange the
garlic, mushrooms, parsley, and cream over
the cod.

2 Bake in the oven for about 30 minutes.
Serve hot with boiled potatoes or
long-grain rice.

nutrition facts	
energy	260 cal
	1075 kJ
protein	35 g
fat	13 g
of which saturated	2 g
carbohydrate	1 g
fiber	1 g
cholesterol	81 mg
sodium	145 mg

baked tuna pasta

AN EXCELLENT ANYTIME, ANYWHERE DISH THAT IS EASILY PREPARED IN MINUTES.

SERVES 4

3⅔ cups dried pasta shapes

FOR THE BÉCHAMEL SAUCE:

2¾ cups soy milk

1 sprig parsley

10 black peppercorns

2 onion slices

2 bay leaves

¼ tsp nutmeg

¼ cup soy margarine

⅓ cup all-purpose flour

1 medium onion, chopped

1 Tbsp tomato paste

1 Tbsp tomato ketchup

1 Tbsp chopped fresh parsley

Salt and black pepper

Two 15-oz cans tuna

1 red bell pepper, chopped

1 cup frozen peas

1 Boil the pasta in a pan of boiling water until *al dente* (firm to the bite). Drain well.

2 Make the béchamel sauce according to the recipe on page 15, but after you melt the margarine in a pan, add the onion slices and sauté for 3 to 4 minutes. Then continue to follow the original instructions.

3 Add the onion, tomato paste and ketchup, and the chopped parsley, and season with salt and pepper to taste. Preheat the oven to 375°F.

4 Add the tuna, pepper, peas, and pasta, and mix well.

5 Pour the mixture into an ovenproof dish and bake for 30 to 35 minutes until lightly browned. Serve hot.

nutrition facts	
energy	700 cal
	2925 kJ
protein	44 g
fat	26 g
of which saturated	2 g
carbohydrate	75 g
fiber	5 g
cholesterol	50 mg
sodium	400 mg

deviled cod with soy yogurt

SERVES 4

FOR THE SAUCE:

1 tsp ground turmeric

½ tsp chili powder

1 tsp English mustard powder

½ cup soy cream

¾ cup soy yogurt

Salt and black pepper

1 lb cod steaks

DEVILED DISHES SEEM TO HAVE GONE OUT OF FASHION, WHICH I THINK IS A SHAME BECAUSE THEY HAVE SUCH A GREAT TASTE. THIS DEVILED COD DISH IS A GOOD EXAMPLE AND THE LACK OF DAIRY CREAM REALLY ALLOWS FOR THE FIERY FLAVORS OF THE TURMERIC, MUSTARD, AND CHILI TO HAVE FULL EFFECT.

1 Preheat the oven to 400°F. Mix the turmeric, chili powder, mustard, cream, and yogurt in a bowl. Lay out the cod steaks and sprinkle the salt and pepper generously over them.

2 Place the cod in an ovenproof dish, pour the sauce over the fish, and bake in the oven for about 15 minutes or until the fish is cooked. Serve hot with boiled new potatoes and artichokes, or other vegetables of your choice.

nutrition facts	
energy	200 cal
	383 kJ
protein	24 g
fat	10 g
of which saturated	2 g
carbohydrate	3.5 g
fiber	0 g
cholesterol	35 mg
sodium	86 mg

tagliatelle with salmon in a white sauce

SERVES 4

5 cups tagliatelle

2 Tbsp extra-virgin olive oil

14 oz boneless salmon steak, diced

2 cups fresh baby spinach

4 Tbsp white wine

1¼ cups soy cream

2 Tbsp freshly squeezed lemon juice

Salt and black pepper

USING SOY CREAM IN THIS DISH NOT ONLY REDUCES THE FAT AND CHOLESTEROL CONTENT, BUT ALSO ENHANCES THE SUBTLE FLAVOR OF THE FRESH SALMON.

1 Add the tagliatelle and 1 tablespoon of oil to a pan of boiling water, cook until *al dente* (firm to the bite), then drain and set aside.

2 Heat the remainder of the oil in a skillet and sauté the salmon for 6 to 7 minutes. Add the spinach and sauté for 2 to 3 more minutes. Add the white wine and continue to stir for 2 to 3 minutes, then add the cream and lemon juice. Season with salt and pepper to taste.

3 Stir the sauce into the tagliatelle, and serve hot.

nutrition facts	
energy	770 cal
	3225 kJ
protein	37 g
fat	31 g
of which saturated	5 g
carbohydrate	89 g
fiber	4 g
cholesterol	84 mg
sodium	159 mg

stir-fried egg noodles with **shrimp** and baby corn in **hoisin sauce**

HOISIN SAUCE IS A SWEET AND SPICY SAUCE MADE FROM SOYBEANS AND OTHER SEASONINGS. IT IS NOT USUALLY USED WITH NOODLES, BUT IT IS SUCH A GOOD ACCOMPANIMENT TO SHRIMP THAT I HAVE COMBINED THE TWO.

SERVES 4

2¼ cups dried egg noodles

1 Tbsp sesame oil

1½ cups baby corn, cut into halves

2 Tbsp sunflower or soy oil

2 cloves garlic, finely chopped

½-in fresh piece ginger, finely chopped

13 oz shrimp

1¾ cups bok choy, roughly chopped

1 Tbsp shaoxing rice wine or dry sherry

6 Tbsp hoisin sauce

4 Tbsp Chinese light soy sauce

Black pepper

1 Boil the egg noodles in a pan of boiling water for 4 minutes, drain well, and sprinkle with the sesame oil. Then blanch the baby corn in a pan of boiling water for 4 minutes, and drain.

2 Heat the oil in a wok or skillet, add the garlic and ginger, and stir-fry for 1 minute. Add the baby corn, shrimp, bok choy, and rice wine, and stir-fry for 2 to 3 minutes.

3 Finally, add the noodles, hoisin sauce, and soy sauce, sprinkle with black pepper, and stir-fry for another 2 to 3 minutes. Serve hot.

nutrition facts	
energy	445 cal
	1876 kJ
protein	33 g
fat	13 g
of which saturated	2.5 g
carbohydrate	52 g
fiber	3 g
cholesterol	96 mg
sodium	3450 mg

mixed **seafood** and rice gratin

I THINK THAT JAPANESE RICE IS BEST FOR THIS DISH, BUT YOU
CAN USE ARBORIO OR LONG-GRAIN RICE IF YOU PREFER.

SERVES 4

2¼ cups Japanese short-grain
   rice, rinsed

3¾ cups vegetable broth

2 cups béchamel sauce

2 Tbsp olive oil

2 cloves garlic, finely chopped

1 medium onion, chopped

1 green bell pepper, seeded and
   chopped

14 oz mixed seafood, such as
   shrimp, squid, scallops, and
   mussels

6 Tbsp white wine

1 Tbsp chopped fresh parsley

Salt and black pepper

1 Tbsp breadcrumbs

1 Cook the rice in the broth instead of water according to instructions on page 14. Make the béchamel sauce as shown on page 15.

2 Heat the oil in a skillet, add the garlic, onion, and pepper, and sauté for 2 to 3 minutes. Add the mixed seafood, white wine, and parsley, and season generously with salt and pepper.

3 Add the cooked rice and stir-fry well. Put the rice mixture in an ovenproof dish. Pour the béchamel sauce over the mixture and sprinkle with the breadcrumbs. Broil until the top becomes lightly browned. Serve hot.

nutrition facts	
energy	800 cal
	3372 kJ
protein	31 g
fat	20 g
of which saturated	6 g
carbohydrate	123 g
fiber	1.5 g
cholesterol	201 mg
sodium	838 mg

marinated **tofu kabobs** with scallops

MAKES 8 SKEWERS

1 lb 2 oz firm tofu, cut into ½-in cubes

16 scallops

FOR THE MARINADE:

3 Tbsp light soy sauce

1 clove garlic, peeled and crushed

A few dashes of Tabasco

½ red bell pepper, cut into ½-in squares

Salt and black pepper

4 butterhead lettuce leaves

Lemon wedges

TOFU AND SCALLOPS ARE A PERFECT COMBINATION, WITH A FRESH SOY SAUCE MARINADE ADDING A HINT OF SPICY HEAT. THIS DISH IS IDEAL FOR A SUMMER BARBECUE.

1 Marinate the tofu and the scallops in the soy sauce, garlic, and Tabasco for 30 minutes.

2 Push the scallops, tofu, and bell pepper alternately onto the skewers. Broil the kabobs for 8 to 10 minutes, occasionally turning them over.

3 Sprinkle with the salt and black pepper, and garnish with the lettuce leaves and lemon wedges.

nutrition facts	
energy	100 cal
	410 kJ
protein	14 g
fat	3 g
of which saturated	0.5 g
carbohydrate	3 g
fiber	0 g
cholesterol	18 mg
sodium	392 mg

stir-fried **tofu and shrimp** with vegetables

SERVES 4

2 Tbsp sunflower or soy oil

2 cloves garlic, finely chopped

½-in piece fresh ginger, finely chopped

½ cup sugar snap peas

2 cups fresh shiitake mushrooms

14 oz firm tofu, cut lengthwise and sliced into ½-in pieces

12 oz shrimp

4 scallions, chopped

Salt and black pepper

2 Tbsp shaoxing rice wine or dry sherry

3 Tbsp cornstarch

1½ cups vegetable broth

SHAOXING RICE WINE IS WIDELY USED AS A DRINKING WINE IN CHINA. WHILE IT MIGHT NOT SUIT SOME WESTERN PALATES OR DISHES, IT IS AN INDISPENSABLE PART OF CHINESE COOKING. YOU CAN USE DRY SHERRY AS A SUBSTITUTE BUT IF YOU CAN GET SHAOXING, I THINK YOU WILL TASTE THE DIFFERENCE IN THIS RECIPE.

1 Heat the oil in a wok or skillet, add the garlic and ginger, and stir-fry for 1 minute. Add the sugar snap peas and shiitake mushrooms, and stir-fry for 2 to 3 more minutes.

2 Add the tofu, shrimp, and scallions, and stir-fry for about 2 minutes more. Sprinkle with the salt and pepper, add the shaoxing wine, and stir-fry for 1 minute.

3 Dissolve the cornstarch in the vegetable broth and pour into the wok. Bring to a boil, stirring constantly, and simmer for 2 minutes or until the sauce has thickened. Serve hot.

nutrition facts	
energy	290 cal
	1218 kJ
protein	32 g
fat	12 g
of which saturated	1.5 g
carbohydrate	14.5 g
fiber	1 g
cholesterol	71 mg
sodium	1587 mg

soy yogurt-marinated
spiced chicken

A HIGHLY SPICED INDIAN DISH. I DEFY ANYONE TO DETECT THE DAIRY SUBSTITUTE!

SERVES 4

4 chicken breasts

FOR THE MARINADE:

1 clove garlic, finely chopped

½-in piece fresh ginger, finely chopped

1 tsp ground cumin

1 tsp ground coriander

1 tsp ground turmeric

½ tsp chili powder

½ tsp salt

A pinch of black pepper

¾ cup soy yogurt

2 Tbsp chopped fresh cilantro

1 Tbsp sunflower oil

1 Score the chicken breasts in a crisscross pattern with a knife to increase the absorption of the marinade.

2 Mix the garlic, ginger, cumin, coriander, turmeric, chili, salt, pepper, yogurt, and cilantro together in a dish and marinate the chicken for at least 1 hour. The longer you marinate the chicken, the better it will taste.

3 Heat the oil in a skillet, and sauté the chicken for about 5 minutes on each side or until cooked. Add the rest of the marinade and sauté for 2 to 3 more minutes. Serve with basmati rice.

nutrition facts	
energy	233 cal
	978 kJ
protein	33 g
fat	11 g
of which saturated	3 g
carbohydrate	1.5 g
fiber	0 g
cholesterol	86 mg
sodium	364 mg

creamed **chicken stew**

I FIND CHICKEN ON THE BONE IMPARTS MORE FLAVOR TO THIS
STEW THAN BREAST MEAT. VEGETARIANS MAY PREFER TO USE
DICED TOFU OR SOY BREAKFAST SAUSAGE LINKS AS A
SUBSTITUTE FOR THE CHICKEN IN THIS DISH.

SERVES 4

2 Tbsp soy margarine

8 chicken drumsticks, skinned

1 medium onion, chopped

3 carrots, cut into ½-in slices

3 potatoes, cut into quarters

2¾ cups water

1 bouquet garni

Salt and black pepper

1½ cups button mushrooms

1 cup peas

2 Tbsp cornstarch

1¾ cups soy milk

1 Melt the margarine in a pan. Add the chicken
and sauté the drumsticks for 4 to 5 minutes.
Add the onion, carrots, and potatoes, and
sauté for 2 to 3 minutes.

2 Add the water, bouquet garni, and salt and
pepper, bring to a boil, and simmer for
30 minutes. Skim the surface occasionally.

3 Add the mushrooms and peas, and simmer
for 15 minutes more.

4 Dissolve the cornstarch with soy milk and
stir into the stew. Simmer for 5 minutes more
and serve hot.

nutrition facts	
energy	470 cal
	1975
protein	38 g
fat	16 g
of which saturated	4 g
carbohydrate	45 g
fiber	6 g
cholesterol	110 mg
sodium	243 mg

braised pork and soybeans

SERVES 4

1 Tbsp soy or sunflower oil

4 pork chops

1¼ cups cooked soybeans*

3 scallions, left whole

1-in piece fresh ginger, sliced

1 clove garlic, sliced

1¼ cups water

3 Tbsp Japanese or Chinese rice wine

5 Tbsp Japanese soy sauce

4 Tbsp sugar

THIS DISH IS STRONGLY INFLUENCED BY CHINESE CUISINE. A TRADITIONALIST WOULD WANT TO USE BELLY PORK, BUT I PREFER PORK CHOPS, AND YOU CAN USE EITHER CANNED, FROZEN, OR DRIED SOYBEANS. IF YOU CANNOT OBTAIN EITHER JAPANESE OR CHINESE RICE WINE, A DRY WHITE WINE WILL MAKE A GOOD SUBSTITUTE.

1 Heat the oil in a skillet and brown the pork chops on both sides.

2 Put the chops, soybeans, scallions, ginger, garlic, water, rice wine, soy sauce, and sugar in a flameproof casserole. Bring to a boil, then simmer for 1 to 1¼ hours with the lid on. Skim off the surface occasionally.

3 Discard the scallions, ginger, and garlic, and serve hot with rice.

nutrition facts	
energy	290 cal
	1219 kJ
protein	25 g
fat	12 g
of which saturated	2 g
carbohydrate	22 g
fiber	5 g
cholesterol	35 mg
sodium	1113 mg

* To prepare dried soybeans: Rinse the soybeans carefully and soak them in a pan containing plenty of water for 24 hours. Then bring to a boil, and simmer for 1 hour before use in cooking.

chinese-style braised tofu and finely chopped pork

SERVES 4

1 Tbsp sunflower oil

2 cloves garlic, finely chopped

½-in piece fresh ginger, finely chopped

1 leek, sliced thin

9 oz ground pork

1 lb 2 oz firm tofu

FOR THE SAUCE:

1 Tbsp shaoxing rice wine, or dry sherry

1 tsp chili bean sauce

1 Tbsp yellow bean sauce

1 Tbsp Chinese light soy sauce

2 Tbsp ketchup

1½ Tbsp cornstarch

¾ cup water

THIS IS A CLASSIC BASIC CHINESE DISH, CALLED MA PO'S TOFU, THAT HAS BEEN AROUND FOR HUNDREDS OF YEARS. MA PO MAY BE GONE BUT SHE'S DEFINITELY NOT FORGOTTEN. IF YOU PREFER A HOTTER TASTE, ADD AN EXTRA TEASPOON OF CHILI BEAN SAUCE. CHILI BEAN SAUCE IS MADE FROM A MIXTURE OF CHILES AND SOYBEANS.

1 Heat the oil in a wok or skillet. Add the garlic, ginger, and leek, and stir-fry for 3 to 4 minutes.

2 Add the ground pork and stir-fry for 5 to 6 minutes. Then add the tofu, rice wine, chili bean sauce, yellow bean sauce, soy sauce, and ketchup, bring to a boil, and simmer for about 3 minutes.

3 Dissolve the cornstarch in the water, stirring constantly to make the sauce thicken without lumps. Simmer for 2 more minutes. Serve hot accompanied by a steaming bowl of rice.

nutrition facts	
energy	250 cal
	1046 kJ
protein	24 g
fat	13 g
of which saturated	2.5 g
carbohydrate	9 g
fiber	1 g
cholesterol	43 mg
sodium	543 mg

stir-fried noodles with
beef and bell pepper
in black bean sauce

BLACK BEAN SAUCE IS A POPULAR AND UBIQUITOUS CHINESE SAUCE, YET FEW PEOPLE REALIZE IT IS MADE FROM BLACK SOYBEANS. MOST STIR-FRIED NOODLES ARE LOW IN FAT AND EASY TO PREPARE—IT IS NO SURPRISE THAT THEY HAVE BECOME SO POPULAR IN RECENT YEARS.

SERVES 4

2¼ cups dried medium rice noodles

1 Tbsp sesame oil

2 Tbsp sunflower or soy oil

2 cloves garlic, finely chopped

½-in piece fresh ginger, finely chopped

14 oz rump steak, sliced thin

1 green and 1 red bell pepper, diced into large bite-size pieces

1 medium onion, diced into large bite-size pieces

1 Tbsp shaoxing rice wine or dry sherry

5 Tbsp black bean sauce

3 Tbsp Chinese light soy sauce

2 tsp sugar

1 Soak the rice noodles in hot water for 7 to 10 minutes, drain, and sprinkle with the sesame oil.

2 Heat the sunflower or soy oil in a wok or skillet, add the garlic and ginger, and stir-fry for 1 minute. Add the beef and stir-fry for 3 to 4 minutes, then the bell peppers and onion, and stir-fry for 2 to 3 more minutes. Stir in the rice wine and cook for 1 minute.

3 Add the noodles, black bean sauce, soy sauce, and sugar, and stir-fry for another 3 minutes. Serve immediately.

nutrition facts	
energy	525 cal
	2211 kJ
protein	32 g
fat	19 g
of which saturated	4.5 g
carbohydrate	60 g
fiber	4 g
cholesterol	78 mg
sodium	1293 mg

4 snacks and side dishes

In this section you will find a selection of more traditional soy dishes that make ideal snacks and accompaniments. Such classic ingredients as sticky beans and beancurd pouches nestle between favorite vegetable dishes such as creamed potatoes and baked cauliflower and broccoli, preceded by a range of tasty dips.

LEFT steamed eggplant with soy and ginger sauce (page 116)

cucumber and tomato **raita**

PREPARED AS AN APPETIZER OR A LIGHT SNACK, RAITA IS DELICIOUS EATEN WITH STICKS OF CARROT AND CELERY OR WITH SOME NAAN BREAD.

SERVES 4

⅓ cucumber, cut in half lengthwise and sliced

1 tomato, cut in quarters and sliced

2 Tbsp chopped cilantro

1 tsp ground cumin

Salt

½ cup soy yogurt

A pinch of paprika

Cilantro leaves, for garnish

1 Put the cucumber, tomato, cilantro, ground cumin, salt, and yogurt in a bowl and mix well.

2 Put the mixture in a serving bowl. Sprinkle with paprika and garnish with cilantro leaves.

nutrition facts	
energy	30 cal
	127 kJ
protein	2 g
fat	1.5 g
of which saturated	0 g
carbohydrate	2.4 g
fiber	0.5 g
cholesterol	0 mg
sodium	3 mg

spicy **avocado** and red pepper dip

SERVES 4

1 large avocado, pitted and chopped

1 tsp freshly squeezed lemon juice

1 red bell pepper, chopped fine

1 scallion, chopped fine

½ tsp ground coriander

¼ tsp chili powder

2 Tbsp soy cream

Salt and black pepper

THE CHILI AND RED BELL PEPPER USED IN THIS RECIPE GIVE A MILD TASTE. FOR THOSE WHO ENJOY A STRONGER FLAVOR, ADJUST ACCORDINGLY.

1 Mash the chopped avocado in a bowl and sprinkle with the lemon juice.

2 Add the pepper, scallion, coriander, chili powder, and soy cream, and mix well. Season with salt and pepper.

nutrition facts	
energy	123 cal
	510 k.l
protein	2 g
fat	11 g
of which saturated	2 g
carbohydrate	4.5 g
fiber	2.5 g
cholesterol	0 mg
sodium	10 mg

creamy **smoked salmon** dip

SERVES 4

4 oz smoked salmon

½ cup soy cream

1 tsp freshly squeezed lemon juice

½ tsp wasabi or horseradish

Black pepper

10 chives, chopped

1 to 2 chives and a dash of paprika, to garnish

I USE SOY CREAM AS A DAIRY SUBSTITUTE IN MOST RECIPES. I THINK THAT, AFTER YOU HAVE TRIED THIS DISH, YOU WILL AGREE THAT SOY CREAM IS ANYTHING BUT A POOR SUBSTITUTE.

1 Purée the smoked salmon, soy cream, lemon juice, wasabi, and pepper in a food processor. Add the chopped chives and mix well by hand.

2 Put the salmon dip in a serving dish and garnish with the chives and paprika. Serve with sliced pita bread or vegetable matchsticks.

nutrition facts	
energy	85 cal
	354 kJ
protein	7 g
fat	6 g
of which saturated	1 g
carbohydrate	1 g
fiber	0 g
cholesterol	5 mg
sodium	482 mg

sticky bean **linguine**

SERVES 4

4 cups dried linguine

2 Tbsp soy margarine

2 cups sticky beans (natto)

2 tsp Japanese soy sauce

1 scallion, chopped

2 tsp bonito flakes (optional)

Watercress, rinsed

1 nori seaweed sheet, shredded

DESPITE ITS RATHER OFF-PUTTING APPEARANCE, STICKY BEANS, OR "NATTO," IS A VERY NUTRITIOUS FOOD. NATTO IS PROBABLY ONE OF THOSE FOODS YOU EITHER LOVE (AS I DO) OR HATE. NATTO USUALLY COMES PACKED WITH A SMALL SERVING OF SOY SAUCE, WHICH I ALSO USE IN THIS RECIPE.

1 Cook the linguine in a pan of boiling water until *al dente* (firm to the bite). Drain well and coat with the margarine.

2 Put the sticky beans with the prepacked dressing, the soy sauce, scallion, and bonito flakes into a bowl and mix together well.

3 Place the linguine on a plate, pile the sticky bean mixture onto the center, put the watercress around the beans, sprinkle with the shredded nori, and serve.

nutrition facts	
energy	537 cal
	2276 kJ
protein	24 g
fat	12 g
of which saturated	1.5 g
carbohydrate	86 g
fiber	8 g
cholesterol	6 mg
sodium	257 mg

stir-fried rice with **sticky beans**

SERVES 4

1¾ cups long-grain rice

1 Tbsp sunflower oil

4 scallions, chopped

2 bok choy leaves, halved
    lengthwise and shredded

2 eggs, beaten

1½ cups sticky beans (natto)

1 Tbsp Japanese soy sauce

STICKY BEANS, KNOWN AS "NATTO" IN JAPAN, ARE ACTUALLY DE-HULLED SOYBEANS, BOILED, AND THEN FERMENTED IN A BACTERIAL CULTURE. EVEN IN JAPAN, OPINIONS ABOUT NATTO ARE DIVIDED VERY CLEARLY BETWEEN THOSE WHO APPRECIATE ITS UNIQUE TASTE, TEXTURE, AND APPEARANCE AND THOSE WHO DO NOT!

1 Cook the rice in accordance with instructions on page 14. Heat the oil in a skillet, add the scallions, and bok choy leaves, and stir-fry for 3 minutes.

2 Make a well in the center of the pan, add the egg, and stir-fry. Add the rice, sticky beans, and soy sauce, then stir-fry for 2 to 3 minutes. Serve hot.

nutrition facts	
energy	503 cal
	2100 kJ
protein	18 g
fat	10 g
of which saturated	1 g
carbohydrate	82 g
fiber	4 g
cholesterol	117 mg
sodium	261 mg

baked **cauliflower** and broccoli

THIS DISH CAN BE SERVED AS A VEGETARIAN MAIN COURSE OR AS A LUNCH DISH. THE SOY INGREDIENTS PROVIDE PROTEIN AND CALCIUM WHILE THE VEGETABLES PROVIDE A RANGE OF OTHER VALUABLE NUTRIENTS.

SERVES 4

Medium cauliflower, cut into florets

Medium broccoli, cut into florets

Pinch of salt

FOR THE WHITE SAUCE:

3 Tbsp soy margarine

⅛ cup all-purpose flour

1¾ cups soy milk

Salt and black pepper

2 Tbsp breadcrumbs

1 Preheat the oven to 400°F. Cook the cauliflower and broccoli with a pinch of salt in boiling water for 3 minutes, then drain.

2 Melt the margarine in a pan, add the flour, and stir quickly. Add the milk a little at a time, stirring constantly until the sauce thickens. Season with salt and pepper to taste.

3 Place the cauliflower and broccoli in an ovenproof dish, pour in the white sauce, and sprinkle with breadcrumbs. Bake in the oven for about 20 minutes or until golden brown. Serve at once.

nutrition facts	
energy	235 cal
	1000 kJ
protein	14 g
fat	12 g
of which saturated	2 g
carbohydrate	19 g
fiber	5 g
cholesterol	0 mg
sodium	174 mg

stir-fried rice with **soy sausages** and mushrooms

AN EASILY PREPARED "ALL-IN-ONE" LUNCH.

SERVES 4

1¾ cups long-grain rice, rinsed

1 cup frozen peas

1 Tbsp sunflower oil

1 medium onion, chopped

6 soy breakfast sausage links,
  sliced diagonally

1½ cups button mushrooms,
  sliced

4 Tbsp ketchup

1 tsp Worcestershire sauce

Salt and black pepper

Chopped fresh parsley, for
  garnish

1 Cook the rice following the instructions on page 14. Boil the peas in a pan of water for 3 to 4 minutes, then drain.

2 Heat the oil in a skillet, add the onion, and stir-fry for 2 to 3 minutes. Add the soy breakfast sausage links, mushrooms, and peas, and stir-fry for about 5 more minutes.

3 Add the cooked rice, ketchup, and Worcestershire sauce, and stir-fry again for 2 to 3 minutes. Season to taste, garnish with parsley, and serve.

nutrition facts	
energy	565 cal
	2363 kJ
protein	23 g
fat	11 g
of which saturated	1.5 g
carbohydrate	92 g
fiber	3 g
cholesterol	1 mg
sodium	1058 mg

spiced stir-fried tofu
and **asparagus** on rice

SERVES 4

1¾ cups short- or long-grain rice

½ bunch asparagus, trimmed and
  sliced diagonally

1 cup baby corn, sliced
  diagonally

1 Tbsp sesame oil

1 Tbsp sunflower oil

2 cloves garlic, minced

½-in piece fresh ginger, minced

4 scallions, chopped

14 oz firm tofu, diced into bite-
  size pieces

1 Tbsp shaoxing rice wine, or
  dry sherry

2 Tbsp Chinese light soy sauce

1 tsp chili bean sauce

1 tsp sugar

AN EASY-TO-PREPARE AND DELICIOUS DISH THAT WILL SATISFY THE
HEALTHIEST APPETITE. CHILI BEAN SAUCE IS A HOT RED SAUCE MADE
FROM SOYBEANS, CHILES, AND OTHER SEASONINGS.

1 Cook the rice following the instructions on page 14. Blanch the asparagus and baby
corn in a pan of boiling water for 3 to 4 minutes. Drain and set aside.

2 Heat the sesame and sunflower oils in a wok or skillet. Add the garlic and ginger, and
stir-fry for 1 minute.

3 Add the scallions, asparagus, baby corn, and tofu, and stir-fry for 4 to 5 minutes.

4 Stir in the rice wine, soy sauce, chili bean sauce, and
sugar and stir-fry for 1 to 2 minutes. Serve hot on rice.

nutrition facts	
energy	530 cal
	2199 kJ
protein	19 g
fat	11 g
of which saturated	1 g
carbohydrate	86 g
fiber	2 g
cholesterol	0 mg
sodium	1000 mg

steamed **eggplant** with soy and ginger sauce

THIS IS A LOW-CALORIE CHINESE DISH—THE EGGPLANT BEING STEAMED RATHER THAN FRIED. IT IS GOOD SERVED EITHER HOT OR COLD.

SERVES 4

1 large eggplant

FOR THE SAUCE:

1 clove garlic, crushed

$\frac{1}{2}$-in piece fresh ginger, grated fine

1 scallion, chopped

3 Tbsp Chinese light soy sauce

2 Tbsp white wine vinegar

1 Tbsp sugar

1 Tbsp sesame oil

1 fresh small red chile, chopped

1 scallion shredded, for garnish

1 Remove the top of the eggplant, halve widthwise, and then halve again lengthwise. Cut the four pieces into wedges.

2 Mix the garlic, ginger, scallion, soy sauce, vinegar, sugar, sesame oil, and chile in a jar, and shake well.

3 In a large pan, boil a little water under a steamer. Steam the eggplant for 15 minutes, making sure the steamer doesn't boil dry. Garnish with scallion.

nutrition facts	
energy	70 cal
	280 kJ
protein	2 g
fat	3 g
of which saturated	0.5 g
carbohydrate	8 g
fiber	2 g
cholesterol	0 mg
sodium	647 mg

creamed, mashed
sweet potatoes with leek

SERVES 4

4 large sweet potatoes, peeled and sliced roughly

¼ cup soy margarine

½ leek, thinly sliced

Salt and black pepper

¼ cup soy cream

THAT OLD ENGLISH DISH, "BUBBLE AND SQUEAK," REINVENTED!

1 Put the sweet potatoes and water in a pan, bring to a boil, then cook for about 12 minutes or until softened; remove from the water and leave to drain.

2 Melt the margarine in a skillet and sauté the leek for 5 to 6 minutes or until softened. Season with salt and black pepper.

3 Mash the cooked sweet potatoes. Add the leek and cream, and mix well.

nutrition facts	
energy	315 cal
	1321 kJ
protein	3 g
fat	13 g
of which saturated	4 g
carbohydrate	49 g
fiber	6 g
cholesterol	34 mg
sodium	208 mg

baked creamed **potatoes**

SERVES 4

4 large potatoes, peeled

1 medium onion, thinly sliced into rings

3 cloves garlic, sliced thin

4 scallions, chopped

Salt and black pepper

1 cup soy milk

2 tsp soy margarine

A HEALTHY, MODERN VERSION OF POMMES LYONNAISE. IF YOU WISH TO EAT THIS AS A VEGETARIAN MAIN DISH, YOU COULD GRATE SOME SOY CHEESE OVER THE TOP BEFORE BAKING, IN ORDER TO INCREASE THE PROTEIN CONTENT.

1 Preheat the oven to 375°F. Put the potatoes and water in a pan, bring to a boil, and cook for 1 minute. Drain and slice the potatoes thin.

2 Lay half of the potatoes in an ovenproof dish. Put the onion, garlic, and scallions on top, and then put in a second layer of potatoes. Sprinkle generously with the salt and pepper, and then gently pour in the milk. Put pieces of margarine on top of the potato, and bake in the oven for 50 to 60 minutes. Serve hot.

nutrition facts	
energy	200 cal
	854 kJ
protein	7 g
fat	3 g
of which saturated	0 g
carbohydrate	39 g
fiber	3 g
cholesterol	0 mg
sodium	33 mg

potato, parsnip, and **soy bacon** rösti

SOY BACON HAS A STRANGE, "PROCESSED" APPEARANCE, BUT CAN BE TASTY AND REALLY DOES WELL WITH THIS COMBINATION OF INGREDIENTS.

SERVES 4

3 large potatoes, peeled

2 large parsnip, peeled

½ cup soy bacon, sliced

Salt and black pepper

2 Tbsp soy margarine

1 Tbsp soy or vegetable oil

1 Put the potatoes and parsnip in a pan of water. Bring to a boil, cook for 1 minute, and then drain.

2 Grate the potatoes and parsnip coarsely with a grater or food processor. In a bowl, mix the potatoes, parsnip, and soy bacon well, and sprinkle with salt and pepper generously.

3 Warm 1 tablespoon of the margarine with the oil in a skillet, put the potato mixture in, and cook for 5 minutes. Then press down and cook over a low heat until the bottom is crisp.

4 Turn over the rösti, slip in the remainder of the margarine, press down, and cook again for a few minutes until crisp. Serve hot.

nutrition facts	
energy	270 cal
	1136 kJ
protein	5 g
fat	11 g
of which saturated	2 g
carbohydrate	40 g
fiber	5 g
cholesterol	0 mg
sodium	71 mg

stir-fried tofu, **green beans**, and red bell pepper in **black bean** sauce

1 cup green beans, cut into halves

1 Tbsp sunflower oil

2 cloves garlic, minced

½-in piece fresh ginger, minced

1 red bell pepper, diced into bite-size pieces

11 oz firm tofu, diced into bite-size pieces

4 scallions, chopped

4 bok choy leaves, diced

1 Tbsp shaoxing rice wine, or dry sherry

2 Tbsp black bean sauce

1 Tbsp Chinese light soy sauce

1 tsp sugar

A CLASSIC CHINESE DISH, USUALLY PREPARED WITH BEEF BUT EQUALLY DELICIOUS IN ITS VEGETARIAN FORM.

1 Blanch the green beans in a pan of water for 2 minutes, and drain.

2 Heat the oil in a wok or skillet, and stir-fry the garlic and ginger for 1 minute. Add the bell pepper, green beans, tofu, scallions, and bok choy leaves, and stir-fry for 4 to 5 minutes.

3 Add the rice wine, black bean sauce, soy sauce, and sugar, then stir-fry for 2 more minutes. Serve with a bowl of short-grain rice.

nutrition facts	
energy	125 cal
	512 kJ
protein	8.5 g
fat	6.5 g
of which saturated	1 g
carbohydrate	7.5 g
fiber	2 g
cholesterol	0 mg
sodium	409 mg

braised sweet soybeans with carrot and **shiitake mushrooms**

2 cups cooked, canned, or frozen soybeans, drained

4 medium carrots, cut into halves lengthwise and sliced into ½-in pieces

1¼ cups fresh shiitake mushrooms, cut into halves

1⅓ cups Japanese fish or vegan broth

3½ Tbsp sugar

3 Tbsp Japanese soy sauce

THIS IS A REALLY HEARTY DISH, PERFECT FOR COLD AUTUMN OR WINTER DAYS. YOU CAN KEEP ANY LEFTOVERS IN AN AIRTIGHT CONTAINER FOR TWO TO THREE DAYS IN THE REFRIGERATOR.

Put all the ingredients in a pan, bring to a boil, and simmer over a low heat for about 40 to 45 minutes. Serve with a side dish of rice.

nutrition facts	
energy	195 cal
	815 kJ
protein	12 g
fat	6 g
of which saturated	1 g
carbohydrate	24 g
fiber	6 g
cholesterol	0 mg
sodium	858 mg

simmered hijiki and **beancurd pouches**

SERVES 4

½ cup dried hijiki

1 Tbsp sunflower oil

2 beancurd pouches, halved lengthwise and sliced

1 medium carrot, shredded

4 Tbsp canned or frozen soybeans

¾ cup Japanese fish or vegan broth

2 Tbsp mirin

3 Tbsp sugar

3 Tbsp Japanese soy sauce

THIS IS A TRADITIONAL JAPANESE DISH THAT USES ABURA-AGE, THIN SHEETS OF TOFU THAT ARE DEEP-FRIED AND FORMED INTO MINIATURE POUCHES.

1 Soak the hijiki in plenty of cold water for at least 30 to 40 minutes. Rinse and drain.

2 Heat the oil in a pan, add the hijiki, sliced beancurd pouches, carrots, and soybeans, and cook for 3 minutes.

3 Add the broth, mirin, sugar, and soy sauce. Bring to a boil and simmer for 20 to 30 minutes or until the liquid reduces by one-third. Stir occasionally.

nutrition facts	
energy	175 cal
	728 kJ
protein	7 g
fat	5 g
of which saturated	0.5 g
carbohydrate	24 g
fiber	1.5 g
cholesterol	0 mg
sodium	834 mg

simmered tofu and **vegetables** in soy

SERVES 4

2 large potatoes, cut into quarters

4 medium carrots, peeled and cut into ⅔-in slices

8 medium shiitake mushrooms, cut into halves

1 medium onion, cut into quarters

14 oz firm tofu, diced into ⅔-in cubes

1¾ cups Japanese fish or vegan broth

2 Tbsp mirin

4 Tbsp Japanese soy sauce

4 tsp sugar

A pinch of salt

1⅓ cups broccoli florets

Rice, to serve

THIS IS THE SORT OF POPULAR JAPANESE HOME COOKING THAT MUST APPEAR ON A MILLION DINNER TABLES IN JAPAN EVERY NIGHT. TRY IT AND I GUARANTEE IT WILL BE MAKING REGULAR APPEARANCES ON YOUR DINNER TABLE, TOO!

1 Put the potatoes, carrots, shiitake mushrooms, onion, tofu, broth, mirin, and soy sauce into a pan. Bring to a boil and simmer for about 8 minutes.

2 Add the sugar and a pinch of salt, and simmer for 4 to 5 minutes.

3 Now add the broccoli and simmer for about 4 minutes. Serve hot with a bowl of rice.

nutrition facts	
energy	240 cal
	1000 kJ
protein	19 g
fat	5.5 g
of which saturated	1 g
carbohydrate	31 g
fiber	5 g
cholesterol	0 mg
sodium	1070 mg

thai-style **noodles**
with tofu and vegetables

SERVES 4

2½ cups dried medium egg noodles

½ cup sugar snap peas, cut into halves

2 Tbsp sunflower oil

2 cloves garlic, minced

2 shallots, sliced

3 small green chiles, chopped

10 oz firm tofu, diced into ½-in cubes

½ cup bean sprouts, rinsed

1 carrot, shredded

2 Tbsp fish sauce

2 Tbsp fresh lime juice

1 Tbsp brown sugar

3 Tbsp fresh cilantro, chopped

2 Tbsp roasted peanuts, chopped

4 wedges lime, for garnish

THIS IS A PARTNERSHIP OF FLAVORS THAT IS CLASSIC IN ASIAN COOKING. HERE IT IS SERVED WITH A DISTINCTIVE, AROMATIC SAUCE.

1 Cook the noodles in a pan of boiling water for 4 minutes, then drain. Blanch the peas in another pan of boiling water for 2 minutes before draining.

2 Heat the oil in a wok or skillet, add the garlic, shallots, and chiles, and stir-fry for 2 minutes. Add the tofu and stir-fry for 2 minutes more.

3 Add the bean sprouts and carrot and stir-fry for 2 minutes. Add the noodles, fish sauce, lime juice, and sugar. Stir-fry over a high heat for 2 to 3 minutes. Before serving, sprinkle the cilantro and peanuts over the noodles and garnish with lime wedges.

nutrition facts	
energy	456 cal
	1919 kJ
protein	18 g
fat	18 g
of which saturated	3 g
carbohydrate	59 g
fiber	4 g
cholesterol	21 mg
sodium	449 mg

deep-fried beancurd pouch **sushi**

SERVES 4

1 cup Japanese short-grain rice, rinsed well

2 cups water

1-in dried kelp, wiped

3 to 4 Tbsp sushi vinegar

1 deep-fried beancurd pouch

1 cup Japanese fish or vegan broth

3 Tbsp sugar

2 Tbsp mirin

4 Tbsp Japanese soy sauce

A POPULAR JAPANESE DISH THAT CAN BE EATEN AS A SNACK OR AS PART OF MAIN MEAL. IN JAPAN, THESE "INARI-ZUSHI" OFTEN FIND THEIR WAY INTO PICNIC-HAMPERS AND LUNCHBOXES.

1 To make the sushi rice, put the rice, water, and kelp in a pan. Bring to a boil, then remove the kelp, and simmer over a low heat with a lid on until the water is almost gone. Turn off the heat and leave the lid on for 5 more minutes.

2 Put the cooked rice in a bowl, sprinkle the sushi vinegar over it, and stir well.

3 Meanwhile, rinse the beancurd pouches with very hot water. Using a rolling pin, roll the pouches on the chopping board, then cut them in half.

4 To cook the pouches, put them in a pan, along with the broth, sugar, mirin, and soy sauce. Bring to a boil and simmer for 20 to 30 minutes until almost all of the liquid is gone, then drain.

5 Fill the pouches with a heaping tablespoonful of the sushi rice and fold to seal. Don't put too much rice in, otherwise the pouch will burst.

nutrition facts	
energy	305 cal
	1268 kJ
protein	7 g
fat	4 g
of which saturated	0.5 g
carbohydrate	59 g
fiber	0 g
cholesterol	0 mg
sodium	939 mg

5 desserts

Choose from this delicious range of hot and cold desserts, cookies, and cakes. Lower in fat than conventional sweets, these recipes offer great taste and variety that can be enjoyed by all the family. From kids' favorites to dinner-party desserts, you need not sacrifice your healthy diet to enjoy this scrumptious selection.

LEFT thick banana pancakes (page 132)

soy **crème caramel**

Butter for greasing

FOR THE CARAMEL SAUCE:

½ cup sugar

2½ Tbsp water

1¾ cups soy milk

5 Tbsp sugar

2 medium eggs

Vanilla extract

A LOWER-CALORIE ALTERNATIVE—SUITABLE FOR SUFFERERS OF LACTOSE INTOLERANCE.

1 Grease the inside of the individual custard cups with butter. Put the sugar and water in a pan, stirring at first. Bring to a boil and simmer without stirring over a medium heat until browned. Pour the caramel sauce in the cups.

2 Heat the oven to 325°F. Put the milk and sugar in a pan, and warm up to 105°F to 125°F while stirring. Remove from the heat.

3 Beat the eggs in a bowl, stir in the warm milk gradually, then put the mixture through a fine-mesh strainer. Mix in the vanilla extract, and divide the mixture among seven small custard cups.

4 Place the cups on a shallow baking dish and then pour water onto the tray to about one-third of its depth. Bake the crème caramels in the oven for 25 minutes. Allow to cool and serve chilled.

strawberry
soy yogurt **milkshake**

WE CAN ALL BE KIDS AGAIN WITH A MILKSHAKE AS HEALTHY AS THIS. IF YOU HAVE A SWEET TOOTH, ADDING A TABLESPOON OF MAPLE SYRUP MAKES THIS EVEN MORE IRRESISTIBLE.

SERVES 4

1 cup fresh strawberries, rinsed

1 cup soy yogurt

1 cup soy milk

3 Tbsp maple syrup

Put all the ingredients in a blender and purée until smooth. Serve chilled.

nutrition facts	
energy	95 cal
	400 kJ
protein	5 g
fat	3 g
of which saturated	0.5 g
carbohydrate	13 g
fiber	0.6 g
cholesterol	0 mg
sodium	20 mg

coconut-milk **gelatin** with mango

SERVES 4

2 Tbsp gelatin

¼ cup water

¾ cup canned coconut milk

½ cup soy milk

3 Tbsp sugar

⅛ ripe mango, peeled and sliced

THE SWEETNESS OF THE MANGO IN THIS DESSERT COMBINES BEAUTIFULLY WITH THE RICH BUT RESTRAINED FLAVOR OF COCONUT. FOR BEST RESULTS, MAKE SURE THAT THE MANGO IS RIPE.

1 Put the gelatin and water into a bowl, and let stand until the gelatin is swollen.

2 Put the coconut milk, soy milk, and sugar in a pan, heat until the sugar is dissolved, and turn off the heat. Add the gelatin and mix well.

3 Place the sliced mango in a 2-pound loaf pan and pour the jello in. Chill in the refrigerator until set, and serve.

nutrition facts	
energy	160 cal
	670 kJ
protein	4 g
fat	7 g
of which saturated	5 g
carbohydrate	17 g
fiber	1 g
cholesterol	0 mg
sodium	21 mg

pear and soy **custard tart**

SERVES 4-6

FOR THE SHORT CRUST PASTRY:

1⅔ cups all-purpose flour

½ cup soy margarine

1 tsp superfine sugar

3 Tbsp cold water

14-oz can pear halves

FOR THE CUSTARD:

1 small egg, beaten

1 Tbsp sugar

Pinch of salt

2 Tbsp soy cream

2 Tbsp soy milk

3 Tbsp syrup from the pear can

Vanilla extract

THIS RECIPE USES CANNED PEARS—SOME VARIETIES OF FRESH PEARS ARE LESS RELIABLE FOR BAKING. THE PASTRY, MADE WITH SOY MARGARINE, IS LIGHT AND CRISP AND, TOGETHER WITH THE SOY CUSTARD, IS LOWER IN CALORIES: ALL THAT ASIDE, KIDS LOVE IT.

1 Make the short crust pastry according to the instructions on page 15. After blending in the margarine, blend in the sugar. Preheat the oven to 375°F.

2 Roll out the pastry on a floured surface. Line an 8-inch removable-bottom tart pan with pastry and prick the bottom with a fork. Score the pear halves widthwise with a knife, for decoration, taking care not to make the cuts too deep. Place the pear halves on the pastry.

3 Mix the beaten egg, sugar, salt, cream, milk, syrup, and vanilla extract in a bowl, then pour in over the pears. Bake in the oven for 30 to 35 minutes.

nutrition facts	
energy	460 cal
	1933 kJ
protein	6 g
fat	25 g
of which saturated	6 g
carbohydrate	56 g
fiber	3 g
cholesterol	63 mg
sodium	204 mg

plum **clafoutis**

SERVES 4-6

¼ cup soy margarine

2 Tbsp sugar

1 egg, beaten

1 cup self-rising flour, sifted

1 cup soy yogurt

1 tsp freshly squeezed lemon juice

1 tsp lemon zest

4 plums, pitted and cut into quarters

Confectioners' sugar, for dusting

CLAFOUTIS CAN BE MADE WITH ANY FRUIT. IF YOU WISH, YOU CAN MARINATE THE PLUMS IN A LITTLE BRANDY TO ENRICH THE FLAVOR OF THIS DESSERT.

1 Preheat the oven to 350°F. Put the margarine and sugar in a bowl and stir well until creamy. Add the beaten egg, a little at a time, and mix together.

2 Put 1 tablespoon of the flour into a bowl and fold in the egg mixture with a metal spoon. Add the rest of the flour in 2 to 3 parts, and fold in. Add the yogurt, lemon juice, and lemon zest to the mixture, and mix well.

3 Pour the mixture into an ovenproof dish and add the plums. Bake in the oven for 25 to 30 minutes, or until lightly browned. Dust the top with a little confectioners' sugar and serve.

nutrition facts	
energy	312 cal
	1318 kJ
protein	7 g
fat	14 g
of which saturated	3 g
carbohydrate	42 g
fiber	1 g
cholesterol	59 mg
sodium	197 mg

baked **sweet potatoes**

SERVES 4

2 cups sweet potato

3 Tbsp soy margarine

¼ cup sugar

1 egg yolk

2 tsp rum

2 tsp soy cream

A dash of vanilla extract

THIS RECIPE RECYCLES THE POTATO SKINS. ALTERNATIVELY, YOU CAN USE A SQUARE COOKIE SHEET TO BAKE THE SWEET POTATO MIXTURE AND SERVE CUT INTO PORTIONS.

1 Microwave the sweet potatoes on high for about 8 minutes. Cut them into half lengthwise and scoop out the cooked potato. Reserve the skins.

2 Preheat the oven to 350°F. Put the cooked potato, margarine, and sugar in a pan, heat to melt the margarine, and mix well. Turn off the heat.

3 Leave 1 teaspoon of egg yolk and add the rest along with the rum, soy cream, and vanilla extract. Mix well.

4 Scoop the mixture back into the sweet potato skins. Glaze with the remaining egg yolk and bake in the oven for 30 to 35 minutes or until golden brown.

nutrition facts	
energy	250 cal
	1.045 kJ
protein	2 g
fat	9 g
of which saturated	2 g
carbohydrate	40 g
fiber	3 g
cholesterol	52 mg
sodium	108 mg

thick banana **pancakes**

SERVES 2

2 cups self-rising flour

1 tsp baking powder

1 tsp sugar

1½ bananas, mashed

1 medium egg, beaten

1¼ cups soy milk

2 tsp sunflower oil

Oil, for frying

Butter, maple syrup, sliced banana, and strawberries, for garnish

SIMPLE TO MAKE AND A FIRM FAVORITE WITH CHILDREN. THIS RECIPE IS SUITED TO ALL KINDS OF TOPPINGS, SWEET AND OTHERWISE. IF THE PANCAKES ARE TO BE SERVED WITH A FRUIT TOPPING, ADD ANOTHER BANANA FOR EXTRA SWEETNESS.

1 Sift the flour and baking powder into a bowl. Add the sugar, mashed banana, beaten egg, soy milk, and oil, then mix well.

2 Heat a little oil in a skillet. Pour 4 tablespoons of the mixture into the hot oil. When the surface starts bubbling, turn the pancake over and cook for a few more minutes, then remove from the pan. Continue until the batter is used up.

3 Dress the pancakes with butter, maple syrup, sliced banana, and strawberries, and serve.

nutrition facts per pancake	
energy	216 cal
	913 kJ
protein	6 g
fat	6 g
of which saturated	1 g
carbohydrate	35 g
fiber	1 g
cholesterol	39 mg
sodium	263 mg

thick pancakes with **blueberries**

MAKES ABOUT
5 PANCAKES

2 cups self-rising flour

1 tsp baking powder

2 tsp sugar

1 medium egg, beaten

1½ cups soy milk

2 tsp sunflower or soy oil

1¼ cups fresh blueberries, rinsed

Oil, for frying

Soy margarine, maple syrup, and some blueberries, to garnish

AS WELL AS THE HEALTH BENEFITS OF THE SOY INGREDIENTS IN THIS RECIPE, THE BLUEBERRIES CONTAIN VERY HIGH LEVELS OF ANTIOXIDANTS. EVEN BETTER, THE PANCAKES TASTE GREAT, TOO!

1 Sift the flour and baking powder into a bowl. Add the sugar, beaten egg, soy milk, and oil, and mix well.

2 Add the blueberries and mix again. Heat a little oil in a skillet, then pour in 4 tablespoons of the mixture, and cook until bubbles appear on the surface of the pancake.

3 Turn the pancake over and cook for a few minutes more. Dress with the margarine, maple syrup, and blueberries, or alternatively with soy yogurt and maple syrup.

nutrition facts	
energy	250 cal
	1065 kJ
protein	8 g
fat	9 g
of which saturated	1 g
carbohydrate	38 g
fiber	2 g
cholesterol	47 mg
sodium	317 mg

RIGHT thick banana pancakes

deep-fried banana and coconut **fritter**

SERVES 4

1¼ cups self-rising flour

¼ tsp baking soda

1 cup soy milk

3 Tbsp finely grated coconut

4 bananas, cut into quarters

Oil, for deep-frying

Confectioners' sugar, for dusting

A BIG FAVORITE WITH CHILDREN AND ADULTS ALIKE. THE FRITTERS CAN BE SERVED WITH A NUMBER OF DIPS AND FLAVORINGS, TO SUIT EVERY TASTE.

1 Sift the flour and baking soda into a bowl. Add the soy milk and coconut, and mix well.

2 Dip the banana pieces into the batter. Deep-fry the banana pieces in a hot oil until the batter is golden brown. Drain on paper towels. Serve hot.

Those with a sweet tooth can drizzle a little honey over the fritters.

nutrition facts	
energy	400 cal
	1652 kJ
protein	6.5 g
fat	19 g
of which saturated	7 g
carbohydrate	52 g
fiber	3.5 g
cholesterol	0 mg
sodium	240 mg

blueberry **muffins**

MAKES 12 MUFFINS

2¾ cups self-rising flour

2 tsp baking powder

Pinch of salt

½ cup sugar

1 medium egg, beaten

¾ cup soy milk

¼ cup soy margarine, melted

1¾ cups fresh blueberries, rinsed

MUFFINS ARE SO POPULAR THERE IS LITTLE TO ADD TO WHAT HAS ALREADY BEEN SAID ABOUT THEM—SAVE TO SAY THAT MADE WITH SOY INGREDIENTS THEY ARE LIGHTER AND EVEN MORE LIKELY TO DISAPPEAR AS SOON AS THEY COME OUT OF THE OVEN!

1 Preheat the oven to 400°F. Sift the flour and baking powder into a bowl, then add the salt and sugar. Add the beaten egg, milk, and melted margarine, mix well, add the blueberries, and mix again.

2 Line 12 cupcake cups with paper liners and place them on a cookie sheet. Pour in the mixture and bake in the oven for about 20 minutes.

nutrition facts	
energy	170 cal
	719 kJ
protein	3.5 g
fat	4.5 g
of which saturated	1 g
carbohydrate	31 g
fiber	1 g
cholesterol	20 mg
sodium	228 mg

brownies

YOU CAN USE ANY CHOCOLATE IN THIS RECIPE. I ALWAYS USE
CHOCOLATE WITH A HIGH COCOA CONTENT AND NO MILK
ADDITIVES. NEEDLESS TO SAY, EVERYONE WILL LOVE THESE.

MAKES 32 BROWNIES

5 oz organic dark chocolate

½ cup soy margarine

1 cup brown sugar

1 egg, beaten

1¼ cups self-rising flour

½ tsp baking powder

1 Preheat the oven to 350°F. Line an 8-in
square baking pan with nonstick baking paper.
Melt the chocolate in a microwave.

2 Put the margarine and sugar in a bowl and
beat well until light and fluffy. Gradually add
the egg, then the melted chocolate. Sift the
flour and baking powder together, and slowly
fold into the mixture. Pour the chocolate
mixture into the baking pan. Bake in the oven
for 30 to 35 minutes.

3 Leave the brownies uncut in the pan for
5 minutes, then remove, and cool on a wire
rack. Cut into squares and serve.

nutrition facts per brownie	
energy	80 cal
	338 kJ
protein	0.75 g
fat	4.5 g
of which saturated	1 g
carbohydrate	10 g
fiber	0 g
cholesterol	8 mg
sodium	53 mg

stem ginger **cookies**

½ cup soy margarine

½ cup brown sugar

1 cup self-rising flour, sifted

⅓ cup stem ginger, chopped

THIS COOKIE MIXTURE DOES NOT CONTAIN EGGS—MAKING IT SUITABLE FOR STRICT VEGANS OR THOSE ALLERGIC TO EGGS.

1 Preheat the oven to 350°F. Beat the margarine and sugar in a bowl until light and fluffy. Fold the flour in a little at a time. Add the ginger and mix well.

2 Form the mixture into walnut-size balls and place them on a cookie sheet. Flatten each cookie down using the back of a fork.

3 Bake for about 15 minutes until firm and allow to cool on a wire rack.

nutrition facts per cookie	
energy	80 cal
	325 kJ
protein	0.5 g
fat	5 g
of which saturated	1 g
carbohydrate	7 g
fiber	0 g
cholesterol	0 mg
sodium	65 mg

apricot and cherry **cookies**

MAKES 24 COOKIES

½ cup soy margarine

¼ cup sugar

1 egg, beaten

1¼ cups self-rising flour, sifted

⅓ cup dried apricots, chopped

⅓ cup glacé cherries, chopped

AS WITH ANY COOKIE RECIPE, THE SECRET HERE IS TO BE WATCHFUL DURING BAKING AND ENSURE THAT THE COOKIES ARE DONE BUT NOT OVERBAKED. YOU CAN TRY ADDING DIFFERENT FRUITS, SUCH AS RAISINS, GOLDEN RAISINS, OR CRYSTALLIZED ORANGE OR LEMON.

1 Preheat the oven to 350°F. Beat the margarine and sugar well in a bowl until light and fluffy. Add the egg and mix well. Fold the flour in a little at a time with a metal spoon. Add the apricots and cherries, and mix well.

2 Place teaspoonfuls of the mixture on a cookie sheet. Bake in the oven for 15 to 20 minutes. Remove from the oven and cool on a wire rack.

nutrition facts per cookie	
energy	80 cal
	335 kJ
protein	1 g
fat	5 g
of which saturated	1 g
carbohydrate	10 g
fiber	0 g
cholesterol	10 mg
sodium	62 mg

raisin **scones**

2 cups self-rising flour

A pinch of salt

2 Tbsp sugar (optional)

¼ cup soy margarine

⅓ cup raisins

1 Tbsp soy yogurt

5 Tbsp soy milk

More soy milk, for brushing

THE SOY INGREDIENTS DELIVER NO LESS TASTE BUT A SLIGHTLY LIGHTER DOUGH.

1 Sift the flour and salt into a bowl. Add the sugar, if using, then blend the margarine into the flour until the mixture resembles breadcrumbs. Preheat the oven to 425°F.

2 Add the raisins and yogurt, then stir in the milk. Lightly knead the mixture to form a soft dough.

3 Roll out the dough onto a floured surface to a thickness of ⅔ inch. Cut into rounds with a 3-inch cutter.

4 Place the rounds on a greased cookie sheet. Brush the milk onto the scones and bake in the hot oven for 10 to 12 minutes.

nutrition facts per scone	
energy	290 cal
	1230 kJ
protein	5 g
fat	11 g
of which saturated	2 g
carbohydrate	46 g
fiber	1.5 g
cholesterol	0 mg
sodium	254 mg

pumpkin **scones**

SERVES 4-5

2 cups all-purpose flour

1 Tbsp baking powder

A pinch of salt

¼ cup soy margarine

¾ cup grated pumpkin or butternut squash

2 Tbsp plain soy yogurt

1 Tbsp honey

2 to 3 Tbsp soy milk

Some soy milk for brushing

THESE VERSATILE SCONES CAN BE EATEN AS A TEA PARTNER WITH PRESERVES, BUT ARE EQUALLY GOOD WITH SOUP AND A SALAD.

1 Preheat the oven to 425°F. Put the flour, baking powder, and salt in a bowl. Blend the margarine into the flour until the mixture resembles fine breadcrumbs.

2 Add the pumpkin or squash, the yogurt, honey, and soy milk, and mix together. Knead to form a soft dough. On a floured surface, roll out the dough to ⅔ inch thick. Cut into rounds with a 3-inch pastry cutter.

3 Place the scones on a greased cookie sheet. Brush the tops of the scones with milk and bake in a hot oven for about 10 to 12 minutes or until the tops are browned.

nutrition facts	
energy	335 cal
	1405 kJ
protein	6.5 g
fat	14 g
of which saturated	1 g
carbohydrate	49 g
fiber	2 g
cholesterol	0 mg
sodium	448 mg

frosted **carrot cake**

SERVES 8

2 cups whole-wheat self-rising
   flour

1 tsp baking powder

1¼ cups brown sugar

1 cup carrots, peeled and grated

¾ cup finely grated coconut

¾ cup soy margarine

2 eggs, beaten

2 Tbsp soy milk

FOR THE FROSTING:

1 cup confectioners' sugar

1 Tbsp freshly squeezed lemon
   juice

1 to 2 tsp water

A HEALTHY, SOFT SPONGE CAKE THAT SHOULD BE A SUCCESS WITH ALL GENERATIONS.

1 Grease and line the cake pan with wax paper. Preheat the oven to 325°F.

2 Put the flour, baking powder, sugar, carrots, coconut, and margarine into a bowl. Mix the beaten eggs and soy milk together, then stir in the mixture. Mix well until the mixture becomes smooth.

3 Pour the mixture into an 8-inch cake pan. Bake in the oven for 50 to 60 minutes. When the cake is done, leave the cake in the pan for 5 minutes, then take it out and put it on a wire rack to cool.

4 Place the confectioners' sugar, lemon juice, and water in a bowl and mix well. Spread the frosting over the top of the cake.

nutrition facts	
energy	480 cal
	2110 kJ
protein	6 g
fat	24 g
of which saturated	10 g
carbohydrate	63 g
fiber	4 g
cholesterol	119 mg
sodium	300 mg

light **fruit cake**

MAKES ABOUT
10 SLICES

3 cups self-rising flour

1 tsp baking powder

1 tsp pumpkin pie spice

1 cup mixed dried fruit

½ cup glacé cherries, chopped

¾ cup soy margarine

1 cup brown sugar

3 medium eggs, beaten

3 Tbsp soy milk

THIS VERSATILE CAKE CAN BE SERVED AS IT IS OR DECORATED WITH MARZIPAN AND FROSTING—AND IT WOULD MAKE A BIRTHDAY TREAT FOR ANYONE INTOLERANT OF LACTOSE.

1 Preheat the oven to 300°F.

2 Sift the flour, baking powder, and pumpkin pie spice into a bowl. Add the mixed dried fruit and cherries, and mix well.

3 Beat the margarine and sugar together in a bowl. Gradually add the beaten eggs and mix well. Add the milk and continue mixing.

4 Gradually add the flour mixture to the margarine mixture, and combine these well. Pour into an 8-inch cake pan and bake for 1 to 1¼ hours. At the end of the cooking time, check by inserting a skewer, and if it comes out clean, the cake is done.

5 Leave the cake in the pan to cool, then remove it and rest it on a wire rack for at least 2 hours before decorating and serving.

nutrition facts per slice	
energy	417 cal
	1756 kJ
protein	6 g
fat	17.5 g
of which saturated	3 g
carbohydrate	63 g
fiber	1.5 g
cholesterol	71 mg
sodium	350 mg

cinnamon **apple tart**

I HAVE ALWAYS LOVED PASTRY DISHES, EXCEPT FOR THE
GUILT FACTOR AT EATING HIGH-FAT FOODS. MADE WITH SOY
PASTRY, I CAN EAT THIS TART GUILT-FREE!

SERVES 6-8

1½ cups soy short crust pastry

3 Granny Smith apples

2 Tbsp raisins

½ tsp cinnamon

3 Tbsp brown sugar

1 Tbsp apricot preserve

1 Make the short crust pastry according to the recipe on page 15. Peel and core the apples, and slice very thin. Preheat the oven to 350°F.

2 Roll the pastry out onto a floured surface and line a tart pan. Place the sliced apples on top, overlapping each slice. Sprinkle with half of the raisins, cinnamon, and sugar, and repeat the process, creating one more layer.

3 Bake in the oven for 30 to 35 minutes. Mix 2 teaspoons of water with the apricot preserves. When the tart is cooled, glaze with the apricot mixture.

nutrition facts	
energy	300 cal
	1270 kJ
protein	3 g
fat	13 g
of which saturated	5 g
carbohydrate	46 g
fiber	1 g
cholesterol	17 mg
sodium	196 mg

index